MW01242294

This memoir is lovingly dedicated to my parents, Sam and Carmelita Maira, who undoubtedly gave me a life of love, values and an understanding of family. And to my son, Philip, who brings pride into my world and an everlasting light that brightens up every day of my life.

I Have A Lot To Say

By Tina Louise Gristina

I was born to two individuals who chose to give me up for adoption. I've never met them nor have I attempted to contact them in my fifty-four years on this earth. I do, however, owe them a thank you for such a selfless act. They probably didn't realize it back then, but they were about to give me the greatest gift they possibly could...a life with a family. My biological parents were not young teenagers as most of us picture when we hear of parents surrendering their infants for adoption. They were twenty-five and twenty-eight years old, both from Kingston, PA. I know this fact because my adoptive mother Carmelita, one of the most loving individuals I have ever known, helped me to get this information.

When I was growing up, my dad Sam read the *Philadelphia Inquirer* every Sunday like clockwork. One particular Sunday there was an article explaining how the Department of Vital Statistics in Harrisburg was, for the lack of a better phrase, cleaning out their files and offering birth certificates to adopted children eighteen years or older. My mom, as curious as I was, asked if I'd like to request mine. So, for the mere cost of five dollars and a few other identifying factors, I sent the request. Granted, this was not how I found out that I had been adopted. I was told at a very young age; I think it was around the first grade or so. At the time, I probably wasn't fully understanding of the word "adopted"or its significance, but in the days to follow, my mother tried the best she could to explain it to me, considering my young age.

In a week or so, I had my birth certificate. There it was, in black and white: my identity. I read it, I saw my parents' names and my birth name for the very first time at the age of twenty. However, looking back, I wasn't really sure what I was supposed to do with this information or what the natural reaction to this situation was, so I filed it away in a desk drawer in my bedroom and didn't bother to touch it for quite a few years. Mom, on the other hand, cried when we looked at it together. I'm not sure if they were tears of joy for me that I now had this information or if she was a bit afraid that I would pursue a relationship with these strangers. I do recall her asking me if I'd like to go further and at least try to find Marilyn and William, but not knowing how to read her emotions, I reassured her that I did not need to do this. I had a wonderful family and the desire was nonexistent.

As the years went by and I finished college, my curiosity about my birth parents began to grow. There were times it was on my mind a lot. I met a young man in college whom I married after four years of dating, and I thought *getting married is such an exciting and pivotal point in my life; wouldn't my birth parents want to know about me?* I read an article once about a support group who reunited adopted children with their birth parents. I remember that phone call to the support group and the conversation I had with the very nice woman on the other end of the telephone. By the end of the conversation, she had felt the need to tell me that these things don't always have a happy ending like we often see on afternoon talk shows. There's always the chance the parents cannot be located, do not want to meet the child, have long since remarried and in some cases have not told their present day family about the past, and of course always the possibility that they have passed away. This was a lot for me to take in. I did not want to experience the heartache that someone who created me would not want to know me, have no desire to know about the person I've become and what my life is like, or not even want to know that I was a healthy, happy grown woman. On the other hand, I did not want to intrude on their present day life in any way. I really had no right to do so. I did not and still don't expect anything from them. They had already given me so much and they didn't even realize it. So with that introduction to my life, let's start at the very

beginning…because at fifty-four years old, I have a lot to say.

❦ ❦ ❦

I am by no means a writer. This is not your typical book…if it

even gets that far. I start out chronologically as best I could, but really I

have so much to say, and my mind races at night thinking of my life and

all my experiences that the point here is to share them and not worry

about specific time frames. If nothing else, I will leave this for my

beloved son Philip to read and to have as he remembers me long after I

leave this earth. So, here goes nothing.

December 11, 1963, a baby girl was born. My name was Barbara

Ann Sutton, daughter of Marilyn Wilson, twenty-five, and William

Sutton, twenty-eight, in Kingston, Pennsylvania. I can only assume that I

was born at Nesbitt Hospital in Kingston because it was the only hospital

in that small community in Northeastern Pennsylvania. For the next three

and a half months of my life, I was in foster care. I have absolutely no

information about the person who took such good care of me in those few months, but thank you. I was healthy and clean, and, by the looks of my countless baby pictures, I was well-fed. My adoptive parents Sam and Carmelita Tuttilmond Maira were married on December 27, 1950. After fourteen years of marriage, they still were not blessed with a baby. Mom told me she had "problems" and was unable to conceive. This is a good place to tell you about my parents, Sam and Carmelita.

Both of my parents were of Italian descent. Three out of four of my grandparents came from Sicily. My father's father was from San Cataldo, Sicily, and his mother was from Sommatino, Sicily, and my mom's grandparents and her father were from Serradifalco, Sicily. My mom was one of four daughters and was an identical twin. Her sisters Leona (her twin), Sara, and MaryLouise were her best friends her entire life. Actually, they *were* her life. Other than me and my dad, I'm pretty sure they were her favorite people in this whole world. My dad had one sister Rose, younger than himself, whom he absolutely adored, and her husband Joe was like a brother to him. Dad didn't have a brother and often used the term of endearment "Bro" when he spoke to Uncle Joe.

I remember all four of my grandparents very well; they all lived to be at least in their seventies or eighties, and my grandmother Maira was ninety-one. I can also say I was blessed to spend my young days knowing and spending lots of weekends with my great-grandmother on my mom's side of the family. I was nine years old when Nonna (in Italian, *Bisnonna*) died. My Nonna was a lovely woman. Her name was Leona Speziale Baiera. She married Leo Baiera, and they came to America from Sicily to raise a family - and raise a family they did. Eight children total. My grandmother was the oldest with four sisters and three brothers. I am fortunate to remember all but one brother, Sam. He passed away at a very young age. I recall spending much time with all of them, very special people, each with a distinct personality. My grandmother's sisters were Lucy, Ida, Grace, and Mary. Her brothers were Michael, James (we called him Jimmy), and Sam.

Lucy was the best baker in the whole family. She had a plethora of recipes, and every time I visited her, she'd have me rewrite her recipes because she liked my penmanship. Lucy was married to Joe Vasta, and they never had any children, she never drove a car in her life, and, impatient to wait for a ride to West Pittston the day I arrived, she called a taxi to take her from Oak Street in Pittston to Spring Street in West Pittston just so she could be the first one there. She was a lovely woman.

Ida was married to Joseph Giamber, who passed away before I was born. I do, however, remember my mom telling me that her uncle Joe Giamber taught her to drive. Aunt Ida was a widow by the time I came into the family, and I only remember her that way. Ida and Joe had two children, Sam and Josephine. She worked very hard in the local dress factory because that's what most of the women did in Pittston at the time. The dress factory was a major form of employment here in our town until probably the mid 1970's. These women worked so hard to earn a measly living; most of the time they were paid according to pieces they sewed or pressed. I'm pretty sure they were there out of necessity, not because they wanted to be. Ida lived with her daughter Josephine and Josephine's husband Patrick Dowd her entire life. Dementia affected Ida, but that was her only health issue for many years, also living until she was in her nineties.

Grace never married; she lived in the homestead with her mother (my Nonna) her entire life. She also worked in the dress factory, and I still remember waiting for her on her front porch of the house on Spring Court in Pittston. My great-grandmother would tell me, "It's almost three o'clock. Go wait for Grace on the front porch." I still remember seeing her walk up that steep hill -- she looked exhausted, carrying her purse and sweater over her forearm. She was my godmother for confirmation, and I was very close to her.

Mary was the youngest of the eight children. She was married to Joseph Coleman, and they raised two sons, Joseph and Leonard. She was the most creative and artistic of all of them. She worked outside the home and belonged to the Wyoming Valley Art League, and because she knew I loved to paint and draw, she took me on a few bus trips to New York and to Washington to art museums. She is the last surviving sibling and still lives alone and takes care of herself at the age of ninety-six.

Michael was the most energetic individual I've ever met. He was always doing for everyone in the family. He was in the service and met a young woman named Raymonde from LeHavre, France. After his return, he completed all the formalities and returned to France to bring home this lovely young woman who would become his wife and an integral part of our family -- a true love story if there ever was one. Uncle Mike and Aunt Raymonde raised two children, Leonard and Leona (Mendelssohn). Uncle Mike did everything fast so my mom gave him the nickname "Speedy." He had such a good soul and a loving heart.

James, or Jimmy as we all referred to him as, was a barber. He will always be remembered as the funny guy in the family. He was always telling us jokes and making us laugh. I suppose that's how he entertained his customers in his barbershop. Jimmy loved to garden. He lived in West Pittston with his wife Sue (Blandina), and they raised two daughters, Leona (Olsen) and Rosemary (Hieronymous), and had the most beautiful roses and flower gardens. He was meticulous with his yard and loved to explain every flower as he took us on a tour of his hard work.

I spent many weekends sleeping over at my great-grandmother's house, the homestead on Spring Court in Pittston. It was cool. The siblings mostly lived within a block of each other, and in the evening my grandmother and her sisters would walk to the house to visit. We loved to watch the good old variety shows like *Hee Haw*, *Lawrence Welk,* and the *Pearl Bailey Show*.

My Nonna was a plump, stocky woman with long, white hair. I remember watching her ritual in the morning, how she fixed her hair for the day. She would wrap a terry cloth towel around her shoulders, wet a hairbrush, and brush through her hair. Then she would wrap it tightly in a bun in the back of her head and push two plastic hair combs on the sides to keep it neat. She wore a dress every day, all day; a "house dress" and stockings.

I still remember how she did her ironing. The ironing board was set up in the kitchen and, because irons were not steam irons in the late 1960s/early 1970s, she would sprinkle the clothes, handkerchiefs, and pillowcases with water, roll them up tightly and place them in a long clear plastic bag and put them in the refrigerator. I guess this was a means of "starching" and made it easier to press the wrinkles out. Yes, we ironed pillowcases; that's how my mother taught me to iron, with pillowcases and my dad's handkerchiefs. She passed away in 1973, I believe. I was ten years old. The Baiera family must have had good genes; they all lived to advanced ages and were the hardest working people I knew.

❦ ❦ ❦

I do not know anything about my grandfather's family on my Dad's side, Joseph Maira. I only know that he and my grandmother Tina Flores, my namesake, came to America as a married couple, settled in

Pittston, and raised my dad and his sister Rose. The only home I remember them living in was 63 East Oak Street in Pittston.

Joseph Maira was an eccentric man, but usually quiet. He grew all his own vegetables in his garden, which took up every available space around the perimeter of his house. He plucked dandelions from the grass and cooked them on the stove. We thought he was nuts, but these days, dandelions are found in salads. He grew escarole, swiss chard, tomatoes, mint (*menta*), basil (*basilico*), and so much more. Grocery stores these days refer to these greens as "field greens" and charge a pretty penny for them. I've been eating them since I was a kid. He would cook them on the stove and stink up the house, and he and my grandmother would fight about it. I can't blame her! He was a vegetarian and preached about a healthy diet to all of us. He loved to read, and his go-to book was about the impact of healthy raw foods on our body. I can still remember that book -- it was titled *Hygienic Review* by Dr. Herbert Shelton.

He was also his own inventor. He put together his version of an inversion table. I remember seeing him hanging upside down on this plank of wood upholstered with a flannel blanket. "Circulation is good for the brain," he said. I guess he was right; he lived to be eighty-nine years old. Other than aging provolone cheese in his basement and selling it around the neighborhood, and spending some time in "college" for making bootleg booze, I have no idea what he did for a living.

My grandmother had one sister Mary, married to Ignazzio Blo, and they had two children, Angelo, my godfather at baptism, and Clara Blo Blackburn. Great Aunt Mary lived her life in New York and then in New Jersey. Their father in Sommatino, Sicily, was a lawyer, an "avvocato" my grandmother would say, and she was his secretary as a young girl. She had no formal education and probably only went to grade school. The story has been told that he wasn't such a nice man, having left his wife and my grandmother and her sister for another woman.

Grandma Tina was all of about five feet tall and spoke with a broken English accent. I only remember her with white short hair and little glasses. I'd have to say her claim to fame was her Italian biscotti cookies with the white icing, playing cards ("scoopa" was a card game she taught me and my cousin Tina Marie to play), and putting up with my grandfather. Their personalities were always crashing; she was a little more difficult than he, I believe. She also lived a long life, but dementia stepped in around eighty-seven years old and she lived the last five years in a nursing home here in Pittston, where I had a part-time job during college. She passed away when I was about twenty-six years old.

❦ ❦ ❦

My parents were very social. They had a group of friends with whom they remained close for almost seventy years. Let's just say they knew a lot of people in their lifetime, sometimes I think more than most. There was one particular gentleman, a lawyer who was a friend of my grandparents, Atty. Ettore Agolino. It was his wife Angela who finally convinced my mom and dad to adopt. I have the original letters in my possession from the Department of Child and Youth Services in Wilkes-Barre, Pennsylvania. The first letter of communication with that office was a response from the woman in charge, typed using an old manual typewriter. This was November 12, 1963. She acknowledged their interest in adopting and told them she would be letting them know in the near future if she would be able to help them. A few days later, on November 15, 1963, a second letter arrived thanking them for completing the adoption paperwork and stating she would like to meet with mom and dad at their convenience in the hopes she would be able to help them.

A few short months later, the call finally came. I was born on December 11, 1963, a baby who needed two loving parents. On March 26, 1964, Holy Thursday that year, and coincidently Dad's birthday, I was officially adopted. My mother always told me that when she called my dad at work (he was working at Lazarus, a department store in Wilkes-Barre) to tell him she got the call about a baby, he asked her, "Well, what is it? A boy or a girl?" She said she was so beside herself that she forgot to ask! So there I was, at three and a half months of age, this blonde, hazel-eyed, chubby baby girl, handed over to my new parents at the Luzerne County Courthouse.

Throughout my life, the story of that day and my homecoming was reiterated to me over and over, by my mom and just about everyone else in my family. My grandmother, my aunts, great aunts, and cousins all had their own story to tell me about that day and the months that followed. This story never grows old to me and I can listen to it over and over again, and each and every time, I get a lump in my throat and find it hard to say any words. Strangely enough, as I'm typing this right now, I feel the same emotions as I have all the times before. I'm not quite sure why this feeling happens to me; it's overwhelming at times, but it happens. I think perhaps I let my mind wander and think "what if"...*what if I was left in foster care? What if I didn't have such a great family (immediate and extended)? What if things had turned out much differently?* The what ifs can go on and on. However, the reality is that I was so fortunate and so blessed to have been given this life that I could cry when I think of it.

❦ ❦ ❦

My parents brought me home to my forever home. They renamed me of course, Tina Louise. "Tina" after my Dad's mother and "Louise" after my Mom's dad Louis. We lived on the right side of a double block home at 116 Spring Street in West Pittston. Within hours the good news spread throughout my family, and relatives took the ride over the bridge from Pittston to West Pittston to meet the newest family member. A home full of excitement and anticipation to meet this "stranger"...I'm sure I felt the love from them all. Everyone wanted to hold me and feed me, *and who was going to be the first one to give me a bath?* I believe it was my Aunt Leona, my mom's twin sister, who had the honor of bathing me. These are all very pertinent things, you know! It's all about the food and love in an Italian family. One of my favorite baby photos is of this day. It's a black and white photo of me sitting up on my parents bed. My mom kneels on the floor with her arms folded on the bed as she leans against the bedspread. We are just staring into each others' eyes, trying to figure it all out. Her smile, even back then, was so wide and full of joy. I was smiling, too. I often make light of that picture and say that I was interviewing her for the job...she got the position. And for the next forty-eight years she fulfilled her duties as a mom. No one can replace that love I have for her and her for me.

❦ ❦ ❦

We didn't live in that first house very long after I arrived. My dad wanted a single family home for us now that we were a family. Fortunately, there was a home for sale right around the corner from where we lived; we literally had to only walk through an alley to get there. It was at this house at 209 York Avenue in West Pittston where I lived my life, from toddler to adult. For my parents, it was the only home they owned until the last three years of their lives. This home welcomed friends and relatives, celebrated many birthdays and holidays and Sunday dinners. It was a home full of music! Always music playing! My father worked in the men's clothing business his whole life until retirement, having owned his own store at 16 South Main Street in Pittston -- "The Esquire Shop," and then renamed "Style Creators" for about thirteen years or so; he then worked in retail. However, his passion was music. His dad bought him a 1938 Gibson guitar when he was thirteen years old and he played until he was eighty. That guitar went everywhere with him -- vacations, family gatherings, and social gatherings. I honestly can't remember a time when music wasn't playing in that house. We had a stereo, believe it or not -- something probably unheard of these days. He played vinyl albums of all his favorite artists: Frank Sinatra, Jerry Vale, Vic Damone, Luciano Pavarotti, Sergio Franchi, just to name a few. He had a band, The Serenades. It was a strolling band of just a few others. There was a mandolin player, an accordion player, and a singer. They were commissioned to play at cocktail hours at weddings, house parties, anniversary parties, you name it. They entertained many throughout the years, playing mostly Italian songs and classic songs of their era. I really don't think there are any groups like them anymore. He worked hard in a clothing store every day and played with his band almost every single weekend. He was a good provider for Mom and me.

My mother was a stay-at-home mom. She was a housewife to the highest degree. She cooked -- oh, and was she ever a great cook and baker! She kept a clean house and was a devoted wife and a wonderful mom to me. Mom was a bit older than my friends' moms, but that really didn't stop her. She was full of energy and vive. She was a Brownie troop leader, and she rollerskated and camped with me. In her early fifties, she even went on a hike one summer day, to Ricketts Glen and Red Rock Mountain. I recently did the same with my son and a group of my class friends. We hiked to the top of Campbell's Ledge, and I thought of her as we made our four mile walk to the top. I believe her greatest pleasure was catering to everyone and making all who came to our home feel welcome and loved. Mom was so full of life, always laughing and making others around her laugh also. She was beautiful, dressed so fashionably, and presented herself so classically. She was loved by everyone; I'm proud to say I'm Carmelita's daughter.

I was an only child. Mom always said she had wished she adopted another baby so I would have a brother or a sister. Having three sisters of her own and knowing how much she loved them and needed them in her life, she felt bad that I didn't have a sibling. I never minded, though. I was so blessed with my cousins that I never gave it a second thought. I was one of eight grandchildren on my mom's side, Tommy and MaryEllen Murtha (Shulze), Michael and Louis Capitano, and Jimmy, Tammy (Penxa), and Amy Fitzpatrick (Warunek), and one of three on my dad's side, with cousins Charles Maira and Tina Marie Maira (Drahus). I am fortunate to have several second and third cousins with whom I remain very close to today.

I was a very shy child. I've since grown out of that! I didn't talk much and was very attached to my mom. I wouldn't go to my little friends' birthday parties without her; she had to sneak out the back door from the party so I wouldn't notice she had left. But I think most children go through that stage. It took almost my entire life until I found a voice, which was just about three years ago! It wasn't that I didn't have opinions or want to speak up, I just didn't do it. As one of my cousins has told me, I was a people pleaser. I guess she was right.

My childhood was a very full and loving one, although strict in many ways. I think it was pretty normal. Every day, I walked back and forth to my elementary school with neighborhood friends, and I spent my summers riding my bicycle throughout the neighborhood, playing with Barbie dolls and swimming in whoever's yard had an inflatable pool, or rounding up the troops for a game of kickball in our street. Our neighborhood street was very wide and quiet, so York Avenue was all ours, we would stay out all day, only stopping in for lunch for a hearty peanut butter and jelly sandwich with a side of potato chips (Charles Chips for those of you who remember those deliveries to the house) and

KoolAid. Then it was back outside for those glorious, warm, sunny summer days.

I doubt if any one of us knew that those truly were the best days of our lives. Carefree, stress-free, and without a worry in the world; that stuff was for our parents. The only thing expected of us was to be home for supper before it was dark. In West Pittston, we had the firehouse alarms that sounded at six o'clock each evening. That was our signal to come home. Dad had a thing about dinner; he was home by six o'clock, and I had to be at the table so we would eat together as a family.

I vividly remember spending summer nights catching baby frogs and putting them in a glass jar (one that was washed out from peanut butter or instant coffee), putting some grass inside, and making holes in the top with a hammer and screwdriver. We actually thought they could live in that environment forever! And lightning bugs!! My gosh, we could spend hours going around the back and front yards catching lightning bugs. Isn't it funny though, that I can't even remember the last time I saw a frog in the yard, and catching lightning bugs is something I never did with my son? He's fifteen, but I suppose it's never too late. He might think his mom had lost her mind if I suggested it, but what the hell, who cares as long as it's fun?

The front porch on my home was nice and big, and my mom always had a chaise lounge, a glider, and some chairs, because all summer long that is where we retreated after supper and on weekends. I can still picture my dad sitting out there on Sundays, relaxing while Mom was inside stirring the big pot of sauce for dinner. And then like clockwork, his very close friend who lived a few houses away around the corner on Parke Street would stroll by and from the sidewalk, motion up to the porch and say, "Come on Sam, let's take our Sunday walk." His name was also Sam and he owned a women's clothing store in Kingston, PA, so they had a lot in common. Off they'd go, stopping along the way every few feet to try and solve the problems of the world. West Pittston is very flat and is a perfect place to walk with century homes, the river, the tree-lined streets, and sidewalks.

By the time they returned, Mom had Sunday dinner ready, and a container of spaghetti and meatballs for Dad's friend Sam to take home for himself and his wife Ruth. She set the table with a tablecloth and cloth napkins, fresh Italian bread, casserole of chicken (either cutlets or marinated with vermouth), spaghetti and meatballs, and fresh "insalata" with greens from Dad's garden. Her marinated chicken was the best! And when we found out her secret, it made sense. A cousin of my Grandmother Nellie, through marriage, Cora Speziale (married to Leo Speziale) lived in Rochester, New York. My parents would visit her when they visited my dad's cousins Felice and Elda in the same town. On one of these visits, Cora gave Dad an unopened bottle of sixty-year-old vermouth, given to her and Leo for a wedding gift. My father drank that bottle very sparingly, yet it was noticeably diminishing. I don't remember how the subject came up, but it turned out that Mom had been using it to marinate her chicken. I honestly thought there was going to be a war in our house! The wine was on the table, and even when I was a young child he poured a little in my 7up to let me taste it -- little did he know I'd grow to love wine!

After dinner on those memorable Sundays, we always had company, whether it was family or their friends. "Come over for coffee. I made a pie," Mom would say to either her sisters, sister-in-law, or friends. Within a few minutes, the doorbell would ring and social hour began. They sat around the dining room table, talking about everything under the sun, with music from Dad's stereo playing in the background and always lots of laughs. They never seemed to care that it was Sunday night and there was work the next day as long as they were together. Everyone lived within a mile or two radius, and some of their friends only lived around the corner, so they'd walk over.

Every summer, friends of my parents or relatives would visit for a long weekend. Some drove in from Lake Hiawatha, New Jersey, and Buffalo, Rochester, or Schenectady, New York. All of them had family here, and staying at my parents was the place to be. There was never a summer that I can remember that we didn't have guests. My mom never tired of entertaining; she was a gracious hostess, and everyone enjoyed her cooking and baking.

❦ ❦ ❦

We were not wealthy. However, there was never a summer that we did not go to the Jersey shore for a vacation. Dad always said that you'll never regret going on a vacation, and it's what makes memories. Off we'd go, car packed to the seams, and not an inch for anything to spare. I sat in the back seat of our 1972 Plymouth Fury, "the Tank," and my feet propped up on a huge green cooler packed with food, because

God forbid we ate in restaurants the whole time we were there. We ate breakfast and lunch in our efficiency room and supper out only one or two nights. The guitar case made the perfect armrest for me in the back seat.

I brought a cousin with me every year, Tina Marie, Donna, Amy, or Tammy. They were my entourage, my sisters. We always had a fun time, and I was thrilled to have a companion with me, especially as I got older. We acted like we were so cool, going to the beach and laying in the sun and walking the boardwalk. We picked out the silliest t-shirts with decals, taking forever to pick out just the right one. We flirted with boys in the game room at the motel, or the lifeguard at the pool...oh, we were so silly.

Here I am at age fifty-four, still able to remember each and every vacation I ever had. Dad was one hundred percent right. I try to do the same with my son. I want him to always remember this time in his life and the family togetherness we have -- it's vital to a healthy and content life. I strive to instill in him values that allow him to appreciate what family is all about. It doesn't matter that his dad and I are no longer married after twenty-seven years; what matters is that he knows he is loved by us. Our family is such an integral part of life and nothing can take the place of it.

❦ ❦ ❦

There were a few years that a bunch of us went on vacation together. The stories that came out of those days are the best! There are even slides (yes, picture slides, that require a slide projector and a screen to view) and numerous photos to tell the tales. There was the year I went to the shore with an ear ache and pink eye and had to wear these extra dark sunglasses with plastic white frames to protect my eyes from the sun. Or when my cousin MaryEllen brought one of her girl friends, and the style in 1972 was to wear bell-bottom jeans and a bandana around our hair. That was the last year that my grandpa Louis Tuttilmond came with us, and he watched the Watergate hearings on TV. We tell these stories forty years later and laugh until our bellies ache and we have tears in our eyes from laughing so hard. No one fought or disagreed, no tantrums, no great expectations. We were all just so darn thrilled to be together at the beach that nothing else mattered...at least, that's how I remember it.

❦ ❦ ❦

Summertime was for sleepovers. We took turns at each others'
houses. Sleeping over the Fitzpatricks was great -- Aunt Mary Lou made
the best pancakes. And at their house I had three cousins to play with,
Jimmy (we are the same age), Tammy and Amy. I played with all their
friends on their hill, Chapel Street, and the days flew by in an instant. At
Tina Marie's we did girly things like trying makeup, painting our nails,
playing tennis at the highschool courts behind her house, and pestering
the hell out of her older brother Charlie. My cousin Donna lived two
hours away in Lake Hiawatha, New Jersey, so we took turns throughout
the summer. Her parents brought her to West Pittston to stay a week, and
then my parents brought us back and I stayed for a week; when we finally
got our licenses, we traveled back and forth between Lake Hiawatha and
West Pittston like it was nothing. Now she and I travel between Pittston
and Ohio where she currently lives, except I take my son with me so he
gets to spend time with our extended family. I want him to know my

whole family and to spend time with them, even if they are second and third cousins. In our family it doesn't matter, family is family.

❦ ❦ ❦

I stayed home with my mom until it was time to attend kindergarten. Back in those times, there was no preschool or daycare. If both parents worked outside the home, which was rare in the early sixties, you were probably taken care of by a grandparent or another relative. I was fortunate to have my mom home every day with me. I went to kindergarten at the age of four because of the birthday cutoff, so I was always to be one of the youngest in my class. Mom walked me to school on that first day to my elementary school on Luzerne Avenue in West Pittston. She was always an emotional person, and leaving me for the first time was very moving for her. She cried, and my teacher Mrs. Fisher, who happened to be a neighbor from Parke Street in West Pittston, kindly suggested she sneak out of the room so as not to upset me. I, on the other hand, was perfectly content. I was there with all the other kids and didn't seem to mind at all, so I've been told. In those days, kindergarten was only half a day long! I remained in that elementary school until the sixth grade. There wasn't a cafeteria in that school, so at lunchtime, all the students walked home and then back for the afternoon. In the winter we wore leggings tucked into our snow boots. By the time I made it to my house, they were soaked! I walked into my house and mom made me take them off so she could put them in the dryer. She was the best! I ate my lunch in my underwear, but as long as my leggings were dry for me to put back on, that's all she cared about. I'd enjoy a bowl of soup (homemade of course) or a peanut butter and jelly sandwich with a cookie or two, and back to Luzerne Avenue I'd go.

❦ ❦ ❦

In 1972, I was in fourth grade. It began as a usual June, summertime upon us, school was out, and the next three months were to be all about fun for myself and my childhood friends. It was an exceptionally rainy month, and surrounding areas were experiencing flooding from creeks and smaller tributaries. I lived one street in from the Susquehanna River. Being so young, I did not realize that state and county offices were monitoring the water levels. I was at Girl Scout camp with my mom and friends, and a bus came to pick us up and take us home. We watched the surrounding cities flooding on television, but I was oblivious to what was happening. In the early morning hours of June 23, 1972, there was a loud rapping on our front door. We were told to evacuate to safer ground. Within a very short amount of time, we gathered some clothes and personal belongings and packed up the two cars. I honestly don't think my parents ever imagined the devastation that would take place next. Dad's prized possession, his Gibson guitar, was carried up to the attic along with all Mom's photo albums. These photo albums held her life. She cherished them and continued to take photographs until she was in her eighties. That particular night, my cousin Jimmy was staying with us; the poor kid was ultimately stuck with us for the next two or three weeks until officials opened up the bridge leading from West Pittston to Pittston, where he lived.

We drove to my parents' friends' house. The Falcones' was sure to be safe from flood waters on Carverton Road in Trucksville. We spent the next two or three nights there, and when it was safe to return to West Pittston, we retreated to the home of another friend of my Dad's, a coworker. We stayed there on Miller Street in West Pittston for the next two weeks or so. As the flood waters receded, Dad had a local businessman take him in his boat to our home on York Avenue to assess the damage. The water was still about three feet high, but subsided enough on our front porch that they were able to pull the boat up to the steps and get out onto the porch and into the front door. We had gotten four and a half feet of water on the first level of our house. Luckily, it stopped there and did not advance to the second floor where our bedrooms were. It was obvious there were going to be months of clean-up ahead. In time, the government, through Housing and Urban Development, issued us a trailer to live in until our house was safe. Other cities around us, including Wilkes-Barre (which got hit the hardest), Forty Fort, and Kingston, were under much higher waters and recovery time took a hell of a lot longer. The devastation was still noticeable for a few years.

I'm not sure I realized what this all meant to my parents. It was the only home they ever owned, and many personal belongings were lost. I just assumed that they would clean it up, repair the damage, and that would be that. But it was heartbreaking. Everyone came to help us, family and friends alike. I suppose we could have walked away from this home, but it was never even a thought to my Dad. This was our family home and we weren't going anywhere. He and Mom worked tirelessly day and night to return our house to the way it was. The gorgeous hardwood floor boards were now warped beyond repair and had to be ripped up, a new heating system was installed, and we got new furniture and appliances. I cannot forget the smelly carp that had been washed in and died on our living room floor -- stinky! But those were just material things. We had each other and the relentless support of family.

During all of this, I watched my parents work so hard and look so tired and worn out, but I almost forgot that Dad was out of a job. He had worked in Wilkes-Barre in a well established men's, women's and children's clothing store, The Hub. It was located on the square and was now gone. *Where are we going to get money to fix this house? When will he get another job?* As young as I was, nine years old believe it or not, these thoughts ran through my head. Fortunately, when the work seemed to be well on its way to restoring our home, Dad found employment in another men's clothing store at our local mall, far away from the Susquehanna River. To say the least, this was one of the most memorable summers in my childhood days.

❦ ❦ ❦

In September, I started fifth grade. I made a new friend over the summer, Maria. She had lived in Wilkes-Barre and lost everything in the Agnes Flood. Her family bought a home on our street, and she strolled down York Avenue, knocked on my door, and introduced herself. Our Dads knew each other, and that was her reason why we should be friends. And so be it. I still consider her my friend to this day.

I had a new classroom and teacher, and we moved about the school for extracurricular activities. I also had my first boy crush this year. My homeroom teacher was wonderful! She was hip! She played guitar and on sunny days took us out to the playground. We sat around her in a circle as she played her guitar and sang. We loved her and she loved us too. She was working on her masters at Wilkes University and, as part of her syllabus, she had to bring two students to class one evening. She chose to take me and my boy crush! It was like a history class that he and I had to take part in. It was very interesting, and I felt honored that I was asked to partake.

Sixth grade was upon us before we knew it. Same school, same kids, but of course new teacher. Isn't it strange how as children we felt that time was moving so slowly, and as adults the years go past in an instant? My father always told me that, and I guess I never believed him or maybe didn't understand the wisdom he was bestowing on me. I always wished I was older so I could wear makeup, wear high heel shoes like my older cousins, or drive. All of those things came soon enough, and now I wish I could slow things down.

Those six years left me with so many memorable times. I had a nice group of friends, some of whom I still keep company with today. Our days were filled with learning of course, but there were fun times on the playground at recess time, playing jump rope, jailbreak, tag, climbing the bars, and hopscotch. We had spelling bees and drawing contests, birthday parties and holiday parties, dressed up in our Halloween costumes and paraded around the outside of our school. Parents came to see us and take pictures with cameras that had a flash bulb on top! Those elementary days laid the foundation for the years to come.

In 1975, seventh grade rolled around, bringing junior high school and the infamous teenage years. I changed schools in seventh grade, and our classrooms got larger. Until then, we had been grouped according to our last name, alphabetically. Now we were merged with children from other elementary schools from our surrounding area, and a lot of new faces graced our classrooms. The way we dressed, our appearances, and our attitudes were changing. All of a sudden I started to carry a purse to school. For what? I didn't have much to carry. A hairbrush, strawberry-flavored lip gloss, a pencil or two, and maybe five dollars in case we went for an ice cream on the walk home. Platform shoes made their appearance, the higher the better. Not one of us could walk straight, but we all had to have them. We didn't have organizers or laptops or cell phones; all of our belongings were kept in a big fat awkward binder, with mounds of loose leaf paper -- your choice, college ruled or wide ruled. There weren't backpacks either. We carried hard-covered books, the binder, the purse strapped over my shoulder to one side and walked in those thick platform shoes, and we thought we looked cool! Kids today would roll on the ground laughing if they could have seen us back then.

I loved school. I loved all of my teachers. I loved doing homework and doing reports of any kind. If I had to think about it, I believe my love for science blossomed in the seventh grade. I was introduced to the microscope, and I still use it almost every day at work. School dances started in seventh grade. Mostly, we went in groups; rarely was it a "couple" thing, since we were only thirteen and fourteen years old. They were held in the gymnasium, and we actually had live bands, local bands that I'm sure were just older senior high school students trying to earn a few bucks. Either way, it was all a fun part of growing up.

I find it difficult to describe how I felt in my teenage years. I was still shy, and something inside held me back from putting myself out there and being able to fit in. I didn't have brothers or sisters to set the way for me; I was on my own to figure these years out. I started out with a nice circle of girlfriends. They were good kids and came from good families. But as time went on, I felt out of place with them. I'm not really sure why, they did nothing to me; it was all within myself. I somehow felt they were moving on and participating in activities that I knew my Dad wouldn't allow me to do. People could only ask you to participate for so long until they stop asking. And being an only child, I preferred a small group around me of only a few. When the group got too big, I began to feel left out. I felt that no one really cared whether I could go to that dance or football game; they would go with or without me. I lacked self-esteem and confidence. I don't know why -- I was book smart, I dressed really nice (thanks to Mom always buying me beautiful clothes; she had good taste), and I was kind. But there was always doubt in my mind. So many times my mother asked if I wanted to have friends over for my birthdays. The answer was always the same for me. No thanks. Why? Because I believed no one would show up, and I wasn't prepared to handle the disappointment. Every year I had a family birthday with aunts and uncles and cousins. They always came and never disappointed me, even though having a birthday in mid-December with bad weather is always risky. There was no such thing as all-wheel drive, front-wheel drive, four-wheel drive, or SUVs. Every winter the garage mechanic put snow tires and chains on our cars and removed them at the end of the season. My family made it for cake and ice cream, and for that I'm extremely thankful. Mom was funny. She'd have the Christmas tree up and decorated the day after Thanksgiving. Why? Because she wanted it for my birthday. She was so thoughtful and giving, and she always wanted the best for me.

❦ ❦ ❦

My teenage years were just like most I guess. In middle school I found someone who I thought could be my best friend for life. She had two older sisters but I don't think she had many friends, just like me. We bonded and spent many years doing the normal things a teenager would do. We rode our bikes around West Pittston, listened to our vinyl albums, learned to tweeze eyebrows, and called boys on the phone. I lost sight of the friends I had for the past five or six years and put all my eggs in one basket. Sure we had a lot of laughs and good times, but there was always something that wasn't right with our friendship. I'm not sure if it was jealousy of me or that maybe she just had a difficult personality. But that personality allowed her to be in control of our friendship and give her an edge over me. For example, shopping for school clothes -- I understood that her parents had to provide for three daughters and I was an only child. But when it came time to show each other what we bought for that first week of school, I remember saying to her, "Wow you got so many new outfits!" Her response wasn't a thank you or one of excitement, but sarcasm. She said, "I can get more because I have to shop in the cheaper stores, not like you, Tina Maira, whose mom can take you to the expensive stores. Not my fault you only got three outfits." As usual, I didn't say anything back, because that was me, non-confrontational. Another time, I admired a purse she had and bought one very similar. She didn't speak to me for days! Lunch time in high school is rough if you're not sitting with your friends. She didn't allow me to sit with her at lunch, and I had to find another table.

We kept in touch for many years after graduation. I was a bridesmaid at her wedding, and she and her husband and parents came to mine. Over the years we exchanged Christmas cards and phone calls about once a month. We were always able to just pick up where we left off the time before, and all we did was reminisce and laugh for the entire conversation. She had moved about an hour and a half from here, but her parents and sisters stayed in our town. A few months after my son was born, I went to the store to buy diapers, and she was walking out with two of her daughters. At first I was so happy to see her, and then I asked, "Why didn't you let me know you were here? We could've gotten together and you could meet my baby." He was born on her birthday, ironically enough. One excuse after the other, and she was headed back home. We said goodbye, but I knew it was the last time. We spoke only one other time, when my mom passed away. She called one evening, we talked about my mom, and we ended the phone call on good terms. I never told her how hurt I was over the years and how I felt she treated me badly. I wasn't that person at the time. I'm different nowadays. I think back over those years, and I regret a lot of the things I did. I abandoned a great group of girls for one person who totally dominated our friendship. I have no ill feelings towards her; it was part of growing up, but I try to tell my son who is presently in tenth grade to have many friends, go out with groups, and do not limit yourself to just one or two. This was the end of the first of a few dependent relationships I have had in my life.

Isn't it ironic how life experiences really do give a person wisdom, and age also contributes? We go through life with blinders on, accepting people and their personalities just the way they are because we care about them, love them, and want them in our lives. But then, we age. And with age we all of a sudden look at things very differently. Maybe it's because we feel our time on earth is limited, and no one lives forever. Maybe it's because we realize we've done it all right throughout our lives, and now it's time for us to do what's right for us as an individual. Maybe we are tired of all the fakeness and facades others think they have to put on to impress. Or perhaps one just gets tired of all the bullshit out there and we just want to have peace and be happy. It takes years to realize this, and when you do, like I have, you finally become the person you were meant to be. Often this means excluding people that made up your life and gave you those experiences, or it means you have changed. I have changed and I'm more "me" now than I've ever been. I preach to my son: be humble, kind, honest, respectful, charitable, giving, and loving. He tells me I listen to too much country music. Teenagers. But he gets it. He is a very bright and sensitive young man, and at fifteen years old, he is mature beyond his years and has the gift of intuition like I do.

I'll tell you another little story about my teenage years. I was going out with a young boy at the end of seventh grade. God only knows what "going out" meant back then. He'd call my house to talk to me and walk over the bridge from Pittston to West Pittston to see me. We went for long walks in the summertime around the streets of my neighborhood, for ice cream, or a movie if our parents agreed to drive us there and pick us up. He was a school friend of my cousin Jimmy, and I met him through him. This relationship, and I use the term loosely because we were all of thirteen years old, lasted almost a year.

I broke up with him, and I hadn't honestly remembered why until a few months ago when I accepted a friend request from him on social media. Wow, it had been forty-one years. He proceeded to private message me. I answered. After catching up, he asked me an odd question. Did I remember why I broke up with him? I thought for a minute or two, and I asked him to refresh my memory if he remembered why. Well, he remembered. I thought to myself, *here it comes, he's going to tell me what a bitch I was and how I hurt him and he held it against me for years.* Much to my surprise, it was quite the opposite. I told him I couldn't see him anymore because he was caught drinking beer, and he needed to stop it and get his life together. Ah! Then my old fifty-four-year-old memory kicked in and I corrected him. I said, "I recall saying I couldn't see you anymore because someone had told me you tried marijuana." He said, "Well…that is what you said, but I just used beer as an example." He told me he owed me a huge thank you, and that what I had said to him made a difference in his life. It was the right thing and it changed him forever. Holy cow! I couldn't believe it. I, Tina Louise Maira Gristina, helped to change someone's life. It must be true, because he went on to a private high school where he was an honor student and currently resides in California and has done extremely well for himself. I'm proud of him, in a strange kind of way. I cannot begin to tell you how good that made me feel inside, that I could leave such a positive impression on someone and alter the course of a young life. It made me smile for a while and feel good about myself. That was the one and only hour conversation we ever had, and I haven't heard from him since. I guess that's why he reached out, to let me know. I appreciate that. So, thank you, JC for reminding me I'm a good person. Sometimes we go through life and never think of ourselves as someone who can make a difference. Maybe we just don't give ourselves the credit we deserve. Even if it seems small and insignificant to us, subtle things can mean so much to another person, even advice coming from a young mind. Keep smiling JC because that's what I remember most about you, your sweet smile.

❦ ❦ ❦

Although I wasn't a popular girl in my high school and my social life left a lot to be desired, I excelled at my school work, and I managed to join a select few clubs. I can't recall doing anything spectacular in these clubs, but I knew they would look good on my transcripts when applying to colleges. I was driving at the age of sixteen and enjoying that little bit of freedom that I really never had. It was wonderful to be able to take the car and go places. Mind you, I did not own my own car; I shared a car with my mom. I'm sure it never entered my parents mind to buy me a car when I turned sixteen. Mom and I shared a 1972 Plymouth that was a god-awful shade of green and had big long bench seats. That car, I swear, was as long as a city block. I took my drivers license exam using that car, and I passed! Hard to believe I was even able to do a proper backup and parallel park. Thank goodness a few years later, Dad bought Mom a new, more manageable car. I happen to be thinking a lot about the expense of driving because my son will be turning sixteen in a few months, and he's done all the research about what kind of car he'd like and even calculates what the car payment will be. Who said we're buying another vehicle? Strangely enough, I don't recall Sam and Carmelita worrying about the expense of another driver in the house, at least not in front of me. I suppose they just knew it was the way life goes. I, on the other hand, am having panic attacks just thinking about it. But after everything else I've endured, this will turn out okay too.

❦ ❦ ❦

I met a nice young man when I was in the eleventh grade. He was in tenth grade, but we had a class together; one of those classes that we were required to take as part of the curriculum. It was a print shop class. We hit it off from the beginning. He was my first "serious" boyfriend. We really did love each other. John was from Wyoming, PA, a town a few miles away, about fifteen minutes from my house. He lived with his mom, his sister, and his grandparents, in his grandparents' home. He was so sweet, kind, and well-read. He respected me and always treated me well. We spent all of our free time together, and I believed he was the one; I think our families thought the same thing. My parents really liked him, but my father had one small contention with him. He couldn't understand why he only wore blue jeans. This is coming from a man who wore a suit and tie and dress shoes every single day of his life; he was in the men's clothing business. This had nothing to do with how I felt about him. He was handsome with blue jeans and sneakers! By nature we tend to be attracted to someone by their appearance at first. I went through many years of my life when it was all about expensive clothes and accessories. I know now that all of that doesn't matter. What matters is what a person is made of. What matters is that they have a good soul, good content of character, and ethical standards. JF had all of these characteristics. We were just kids, and we looked cool in our jeans! And now, in 2018 I have learned that jeans are acceptable anywhere you go. Sam wouldn't be too happy about that!

We enjoyed going to our proms and movies and spending holidays together. Our summers seemed to go on forever. He filled the friendships I was lacking with other girls. Our love lasted for four years. We saw each other graduate high school and go on to college and often studied together. I was guilty of always wanting to be with him. He wanted to be with me too, but every once in a while he wanted to spend time with his guy friends. I wasn't the most understanding when it came to this. Oh, the guilt I would lay on him. He had patience, though, and I can't remember a time that we were angry with each other. After four years of being a couple, John and I broke it off. I was a junior at the University of Scranton, and he had transferred to Penn State University main campus three hours away. I saw that this was not going to work. My father would never allow me to go to see him; he was too strict about that. I realized that to expect him to come home every weekend to be with me was way too much to ask. These were to be the best times of our lives, and we both had to experience college life and spread our wings. We ended things on a good note, although I wasn't too sure of that at the time.

Since 1984, I had only seen him one time in a grocery store of all places, until about three years ago. That was in church at a mutual friend's funeral mass. As I got dressed to go to church that morning, I hoped I would see him. He was much closer to the deceased gentleman than I was, so the chances were pretty great. He approached me, and we talked about the old times, and he bragged about my mom and her cooking and told me how much he adored her. She loved him! He could see my eyes filling up and how emotional I was just talking about her. He had sent me a sympathy card when she passed away. I told him about my separation from my husband and that divorce was inevitable. He gave me a great big warm embrace, told me how special I was and that those four years with me meant so much to him. He told me he loved me back then and that I will always have a place in his heart. These sentiments came at the right time. I will never forget those words or how kind his eyes were when we were talking. Looking back, I realize what an incredible man he matured into; his wife should consider herself very lucky. You'll always have a place in my heart too, JF.

In December I was with a close circle of friends, including one who is a judge. For the heck of it, I asked him how difficult it would be to see my adoption case. He gave me the name of an attorney that specializes as an adoption liaison. I held onto that information for months, and one afternoon as I was writing this book, I thought to myself, *I'm already typing, perhaps I'll type a letter to this attorney and see how far I can get.* I began by telling her how I obtained her name and information and that I have some information about my adoption but I'd like to know more. About ten days passed and I heard back from her. She acknowledged my request and told me she would find out what information she can give me and get back to me. Two weeks later she told me that my biological parents were indeed married at the time of my birth and adoption -- something I did not know for certain because only my mother's maiden name was on my birth certificate. Even though my birth name had my father's last name, I did not know for sure the circumstances. She proceeded to inform me that although they were married at the time of their relinquishment and my adoption, they had not lived together "for several years." There was no testimony offered on the issue of whether William was acknowledging or disputing paternity. She said, both Mr. and Mrs. Sutton testified that they were relinquishing their parental rights as they were unable to care for me and wanted me to have a better life, which I think is what most biological parents say when they choose to give their baby up for adoption. There was no further information such as health, genetics, or ethnicity within the records. There may have been more information, but she was unable to locate either one of them and therefore could not get the permission she needed to do so.

This opened up a whole new can of worms. Married, not living together for several years, pregnant, me, adoption. What exactly had happened? Is he even my biological dad? He neither admitted nor denied paternity. Was William in the courtroom only for the sole purpose to stand by Marilyn? I'll never know for certain. This is not the end of this part of my life story. Now more than ever, I will continue to research and put the puzzle pieces together. I still have no intention of making contact with anyone, but I would like to come full circle and complete my story.

I often wonder why some people treat others the way they do. Even good, upstanding, educated, successful, ethical people sometimes take out their internal conflicts and issues on those that have stood by them and tried to maintain a decent relationship with them. Perhaps it comes down to familiarity -- as Mom said, "you know, we often hurt the ones we love." It's unfair, hurtful, and frustrating. Although I realize we are not made to change others, I often keep trying. I am a good judge of character, and I see through people's facades almost from the minute I meet them. I find it sad that they just don't know how to be themselves. What a grueling and exhausting task it must be to constantly be "on" for the public eye, even for friends and family. So often, these same people who exhibit fakeness in public are unhappy in their personal life. Don't they realize that just being who you are will attract people? Ironically, relationships fail, marriages end, and friendships falter. Sometimes they lose the people that mattered most in their life. I have found that once I decided to be calm and myself and unafraid of speaking my mind, I became happier. I actually started having fun again! What a joy and blessing. My family and friends noticed the change and were thrilled to have the old Tina back. I was often available for people to walk over me and be condescending to me because of my demeanor. I've changed a lot over the past few years and this doesn't seem to be an issue any longer.

I have also felt the absence of apology. It is so difficult for some to apologize for their behavior. What is so hard about saying those two words? "I'm sorry" can mean so much. Saying those words is acknowledging you hurt someone's feelings and be the first step to repairing that hurt.

❦ ❦ ❦

I was an A student all through high school and was inducted into the National Honor Society in my junior year. I loved doing homework and assignments. Kind of weird, I know, but it's the truth. Knowing I was making my mom and dad proud made me feel good. I knew I was going to college, but I never even asked my parents about going away for school. I assumed two things: They were too strict to allow me to go, and maybe they couldn't afford it. I loved science, biology, and chemistry. With my grades and interest in biology, I decided I wanted to go to medical school and specialize in pediatrics. I have always loved children, and I was responsible enough to babysit at a fairly young age, maybe twelve. I applied to a local university, the University of Scranton, which at the time had an excellent reputation for their Biology (professional) program and medical school placement in the upper 90th percentile. I applied and I was accepted. There was my future for the next four years at least. Many of us from my high school, Wyoming Area, also attended "Scranton U." We put our heads together and came up with a carpool schedule that was more complicated than Einstein's Theory of Relativity. We did this for four years, although I met my ex-husband in my junior year and on occasion our schedules coincided and we rode together.

I was in no way prepared for the journey I was about to begin, for the intense workload or studying that was bestowed upon me. I was challenged with others that were privileged to have attended private college preparatory high schools and had a head start on the course curriculums. I was at a high disadvantage; I wasn't taught the correct way to study in school, and I never had to study all that hard to get a good grade, but this was a bear! After my first semester in 1981, I cried to my parents, doubting I could do it for four years. My concerns were legitimate. Failure was very foreign to me. I couldn't possibly disappoint my parents or not make them proud. My parents and I made an appointment with the head of the nursing program, thinking maybe that was the road to take. I'd still be in the sciences and still be able to help others. I thought, *certainly the program would be easier than pre-med.* I realize now, a nurse's job is very demanding, and I have the highest regard for what they do. As I think back, who in their right state of mind knows what they are meant to do for their entire working life at eighteen? I commend those that did, but it's not often the case. Maybe colleges and universities should offer a free one year opportunity to experience a little bit of every course as an introduction so these young students can decide on their own what they'd like to study, instead of listening to guidance counselors in high school that were near the age of retirement and told us to go with what the trend was at that time. In my time, it was the sciences and computers. I'm attempting to write a book here in 2018 at the age of fifty-four...maybe I should have read more and tried to be a writer. After a long talk, we decided I would stay right where I was.

1985, I graduated with a BS in Biology. I knew darn well that my grades were not good enough to get into a medical school of any kind, so I didn't know what to do with it. I went to a professional company to assist me with a resume and started looking for a job in research laboratories and pharmaceutical sales. I went on a few interviews, but had no success. Everyone wanted experience, but how on earth could I get the experience if no one was willing to hire me? I continued working at the nursing home where I had worked weekends throughout my college years, only this time as a private duty aide. The money was cash, so I didn't have to ask my mom and dad for spending money. The work was back-breaking and tiring. After five years, I would wonder to myself, *what the hell am I still doing here?*

I looked into a Medical Technology program that utilized the three hospitals in Scranton, PA. This one year internship program would use all my credits from biology, chemistry, and physics. Mornings were spent doing rotations in all the departments of the hospital laboratory, and after lunch we had lectures. After one long year, I graduated, this time as a Medical Technologist. I got a job two weeks later at The American Red Cross Blood Services in their infectious disease laboratory. I worked three different capacities while there. After five years in the laboratory, I started an Intraoperative Autologous Transfusion program from the ground up. With the assistance of my coworker, a registered nurse, we created pamphlets and a price list and attended monthly transfusion committee meetings with surgeons to sell our service. For the last seven years there, I worked in the Quality Assurance Department.

I ended my fifteen-year career after the birth of my son. I took a six-month maternity leave; it was a long and emotional road becoming a mother, and I wanted to spend every minute of my day with him. Weeks prior to returning to work at the Red Cross Blood Services, I met with the Human Resources Director to discuss coming back at a part time capacity or perhaps working longer days so I could have a few days off during the week, or entertain the idea of job-sharing with another part time employee. She refused. My position required forty hours a week and there were no other options other than to return to work and assume my responsibilities in the quality assurance department or submit my resignation. I remember that day so clearly. I almost didn't make it out to my car in time for a tearful meltdown. I had given this company fifteen years of my life. Dedicated and dependable and they wouldn't bend one inch to work with me. I called my husband when I got in my car and cried all the way home from Wilkes-Barre to Pittston.

In November 2002, I returned to work. I had to leave my baby with my in-laws or my parents. After several weeks we realized it was much easier to leave him with my in-laws, as they lived right next door. My parents spent their winters in Clearwater, Florida every year, and they were much older than my husband's parents and I think it was tiring for them. I stayed at the Red Cross, actively looking for a part-time job so I could be with Philip. One day there was a seminar at the blood center and area technologists attended. I saw a familiar face in the crowd. Debbie was a technologist at one of the hospitals where I had done my internship in 1987. I asked her if there were any positions available, and she told me only the second shift and part time. I gave her my resume, and a week later I received a call from Joe, the laboratory director at Community Medical Center in Scranton. I resigned from the Red Cross, and in May of 2003, I started work at CMC. I am still employed there today, fifteen years later.

At forty years old I learned hospital laboratory work all over again. It was not a simple task, but we find strength and ability when the outcome will be of great benefit to us.

My son Philip is fifteen years old as I write this. He is a sophomore in a college preparatory school, Wyoming Seminary, here in Kingston, Pennsylvania. He has the most beautiful red hair and the darkest brown eyes and the fairest skin! Philip was born in June of 2002. It took many years and many tears to finally have a baby. We were married almost fourteen years before Philip was born. In the sixth year of our marriage, we decided we would try to have a baby. The first five years, we adjusted to married life, to living together (we both had lived at home until the day of our wedding), and to supporting ourselves. We both worked full time and spent our leisure time with friends. We enjoyed road trips, family gatherings, shopping, and having fun. We were young, twenty-four years old when we married. We rented one half of a double block home on Wyoming Avenue in West Pittston. The owner lived on the other side. He was a longtime family friend of my grandparents and my parents and just so happened to have been the attorney for my parents for my adoption. Living there was like living next to family. The house was spacious, with the ten foot ceilings, window seats, hidden envelope doors, beautiful carved woodwork, and lots of floor-to-ceiling windows. We were living it up in a big way for two kids. I used to say that those first five years of our marriage living there were the happiest. We had a gorgeous dining room with a huge built-in china closet with bevelled glass doors. We did a lot of entertaining in that house, many dinners and happy times spent with our family and friends. We had some rocky times even in the beginning, in that home too. Newlywed tiffs I guess, but they were more than likely a sign of what the future would hold. I know we loved each other back in those years, but fast forward twenty-five years and a divorce two years ago, and I have doubts. When you go through the hurt and resentment and anger of a divorce, you find yourself doubting everything and maybe it's as simple as that, just doubts. We lived in that Victorian beauty for five years and then bought a home on Elizabeth Street in Pittston. I cried to leave West Pittston, the little town I grew up in with my parents only two streets over. I didn't want to move, but our landlord was elderly and not in the best health. The writing was on the wall that he would probably move to downsize and sell the home. It was very affordable for us, but the future of who would own the house and what our rent would be was uncertain. We purchased my husband's grandparents' home next door to my in-laws. I cried to my dad that I didn't want to move, and he told me,

"Just go. It's a starter home. You'll be fine; it's only across the bridge." That was in 1993, and I'm still here in that starter home in 2018. So much for THAT theory, Sam Maira.

Around 1994 we decided to try to start a family. We tried on our own for one year. That's what the doctors all say to do, try for one year. I was thirty years old, and with no success, I sought out help from my gynecologist. I started on fertility medication and after a few months, I was pregnant. All I wanted was to be a mom. Isn't that the way it should be? I was married to a man I loved, we were both employed, we had a home of our own, and we were good people. We were so excited to tell our family, our friends, and our coworkers. My due date was June 6, 1996...6/6/96. That's how I'll always remember that day. I recall telling one of the representatives from a company we bought our instruments from in the lab at the Red Cross, that I was pregnant. She asked me how far along I was, and I told her almost three months. Her response startled me and actually made me sick to my stomach. She said, "Only three months and you're telling people? Anything can happen." I was so taken back by her remark that I wanted to cry. *How could she say such a stupid remark to me? Didn't she know how happy I was, and that it took awhile for me to actually get pregnant?* Who says things like that to someone who is standing there with a big smile and hope and glistening stars in their eyes? Sandy did. I resented her from that day forward, and every time she came to our laboratory, I couldn't even make eye contact with her.

In November, I had a miscarriage, one of two. I was crushed; we were crushed. For the first time ever, I saw my husband cry. I knew something was wrong one early morning as I was getting ready for work. I called off sick and waited for my doctor's office to open. We went in for an examination. He told us very gently that I had lost the baby. He directed us to go home and come back to the hospital in a few hours so he could make arrangements to reserve an operating suite. I needed to have a D&E. I knew a few of the nurses in the OR, one was a best friend of my cousin Mary Ellen and the other was my husband's cousin's wife. Both held my hand as they wheeled me in, tears streaming down my cheeks. I felt I had lost all my hopes to be a mother. In the recovery room, I heard Al on the phone with my mother. He could hardly get the words out. We came home late in the day. I put my pajamas on and went to sleep on the couch. Funny, I don't remember how much we talked that night. I think we were so sad that there were no words. I stayed home one week from work. I didn't know how I was going to face my coworkers. Undoubtedly they would approach me to offer support, and I didn't want to break down in front of them. Most family and friends were very supportive, and we received many phone calls and cards and even flowers. I remember returning to the gym and my trainer hugging me. My friends from the gym had a beautiful floral arrangement waiting for me. I told her that I was done trying to get pregnant, that it didn't matter to me anymore. What a huge mistake that would've been. Those gestures meant a lot to me. My sister-in-law was also pregnant. Their son was due around Thanksgiving. Two weeks after my miscarriage, my nephew was born. First grandchild, first nephew. Born at the same hospital I had just been at two weeks prior. I remember getting the call at work, that they were all there to see the new baby. "You are going to come here on your way home, right?" *Why in hell would I want to go there in my emotional state?* It was expected of me. I went because I'm a people pleaser and at that time in my life and for decades to follow, I always put others ahead of myself. I went with a heavy heart that I wore on my sleeve. I couldn't say a word while I was there. I didn't want to hold the baby, and quite honestly I couldn't wait to get the hell out of there. *How am I ever going to get over this?* Outside the hospital, my brother- in-law's mother hugged me and whispered in my ear, "I know you are hurting and I'm so sorry for your loss, but you are blessed Tina, and I know you will be a mom. And you will be a great mom." Those are words I'll never forget. She was the only one in that room that offered some comfort to me. A month later, I stood at the altar in our church baptizing my nephew. You can see the anguish on my face in the photographs. I was back on fertility drugs, but they were not working. I had ultrasounds once a week, ovulation kits every month, doctor's appointments that I started going to alone because they were so often. It was very emotionally and physically draining for us, but I wasn't giving up. Going through this time in my life, I thought, *who of my friends or family have gone through this sadness? Did I know if they did? And if I did, please tell me that I reached out to them and offered some kind words to them.*

Here we are many years later, and I love my nephews with all of my heart. My sister-in-law, Lisa and her husband, Jeff have done a magnificent job raising these two young men. The oldest graduated from Columbia University and is successfully working in Manhattan. His brother will graduate this year from the same college preparatory high school as my son and will be attending Harvard University, and I'm positive he will go on to do great things with his life. They are handsome, intelligent, respectful, kind, and considerate young men. I'm so very proud of both Matthew and Michael. We don't get to see each other often since my divorce and I can appreciate how busy life gets at times. I only hope they know that no matter what, I am still their godmother and I love them dearly. I think we go through life and think, *Oh, that'll never happen to me.* And it could apply to all situations -- loss of a family member, leaving a job, natural disaster and losing your personal possessions, divorce. Well, it could absolutely happen to anyone. I should know, all of those things have happened to me. I remember talking to the nurse practitioner in my doctor's office in the weeks following my miscarriage. I was having a hard time dealing with some family members who did not acknowledge our loss, and I was hurt. I asked her if I was being silly because I was three months along. Maybe that's not a real loss for some people looking in from the outside. She told me to talk to those individuals and let them know how I feel. One night, I was home alone and still weepy, but I got up the courage to call my mother-in-law and asked her to please come over and sit with me. We sat, just the two of us, and I expressed how hurt I was that some family members had not reached out to me. She cried. She tried to explain the best she could. Perhaps this never happened to them, and they didn't know what to say. I cried too. I told her all they had to do was say something, anything.

Many years followed and still we were not parents. I couldn't bring myself to go to baby showers or Easter egg hunts -- the list goes on. If you have experienced this, I have no doubt that you can relate. I couldn't even be happy when my sister-in-law was pregnant for the second time, or even for my cousin who is like a sister to me. This went on for years, eight years to be exact. Every day in the newspaper or on the evening news, I heard stories about children being abused or murdered, and there we were, good people who could provide a home, family, and a good life for a baby, but God chose to give one to those in the headlines instead. *How could He be so cruel?* I must have asked myself that hundreds of times. Meanwhile it seemed like everyone around us was becoming parents. We endured medications, shots, surgeries, tests, specialists in Hershey Hospital. We tried all we could financially. I had a second miscarriage along the way. I was only a few weeks along this time, and I only confided in two or three people when this happened. I took a break for a few months from all treatments, switched doctors, and hoped it would happen naturally. My new doctor looked at my stack of records. I sat across from his desk as he leafed through the mounds of paper sent over from my previous doctor. He told me he saw absolutely nothing wrong with me physically. I think his exact words were, "Other than a novena to St. Ann, you should be able to get pregnant." I took a break from all medications and let my body and mind recover. I continued to work really hard at the gym with my trainer, and I was beginning to feel good about myself again. It was possible for me to get pregnant again, but staying pregnant was the hurdle we had to get over. And hopefully, my marriage could stay together and weather the storm, because the pressure of all of this was extreme and tensions were high at times. We continued to try to get pregnant, this time on our own. No outside intervention, no medications, no shots, and no weekly visits to the OB/GYN. Late September of 2001, I went for bloodwork at my family physician's laboratory. I had a gut feeling I might have been pregnant. A day or two later, I got a call from the nurse in his office, someone I've known for years from being his patient since high school. She almost couldn't speak. I think she was as elated as I would soon be when she said the words, "You're pregnant." I was home alone and speechless. I just kept asking her if she was sure. My husband and I made the decision to tell no one. Not one friend, not one parent, not one family member. We did tell our priest; we asked him to please pray for us.

The next nine months were so wonderful. I felt good and I absolutely loved being pregnant, every single day. I was thirty-eight years old and considered high risk, but I had no complications, and I considered every day a blessing from God. Physically I was in great shape before becoming pregnant, and I think that helped a lot considering my age. I had no other health problems and still don't at the present time -- pretty good for fifty four! If I had to sum up how I felt during those months, I was genuinely happy every single minute of every single day. Nothing bothered me, and for the first time (and probably the last) I had no worries. I cherished the fact that I had a baby growing inside and that our dream had finally come true. I was going to be a mom, a mother, a role model. We didn't tell anyone until I had a special ultrasound done at a hospital about an hour from home. I was about four months pregnant. The baby looked healthy and all his parts were intact and growing as he should be. We came home from Allentown that evening and went to both of our parents' homes and told them the good news. Oh the joy! When we told my mom and dad, they cried. I think my father was at a loss for words for the first time in his life, but I could see the joy in his big blue eyes. After the initial shock, my mom asked if it was okay to tell her sisters. And the two things I remember them saying were this: Dad: "I knew something was up because you didn't have a glass of wine with Sunday dinner." Mom: "And is that why you haven't colored your hair? Your gray roots are a mess." All I could do was laugh. I made an appointment the next day. She was always a riot.

It was the week of Christmas by this time. I hadn't told any of my coworkers at the Red Cross. I sat at my computer in my office and composed a very sweet announcement for my friends. I said something to this effect: "Christmas is the season of giving, love, and joyful blessings, and it is with tremendous love that I am sharing with you the joyful news that Al and I have been blessed with a little boy expected to be part of our

71

family in June of 2002." Within minutes, people flooded my office with hugs and kisses and tears! They knew. They knew that we had waited so long and tried so hard to be parents, and if everything was to go as God had planned for us, it would become a reality.

Months went by and my body was changing. Everything was getting bigger! I didn't care at all. I loved buying new clothes. I wanted to be stylish even though my thighs were touching for the first time in my life and my breasts…well, let's just say, they were pretty darn noticeable, also for the first time in my life. I pampered myself and ate really healthy, following the guidelines the OB/GYN office had given me. I got plenty of rest and felt great every day. My visits to the doctor were good. The staff made me feel so special because they knew my history. Everything was progressing like a textbook pregnancy. I was so grateful. During this same time, my younger cousin Tammy was also pregnant with her first child. We are only three years apart. We compared notes often; it was wonderful to go through this special time with her. Her son was born in May and our son was born in June. Her sister, Amy, my younger cousin of six years, already had two boys and was like our personal guidance counselor. Amy hosted a joint baby shower for the two of us with all of our family members present. It was so beautiful. I had four baby showers. Amy had that one, my cousin Tina Marie with my mom and her mom Rose held a shower at her home with my friends from Red Cross and our family, my sister-in-law hosted at her home with Al's side of the family and my friends, and my coworkers had one at work. I was so blessed with the beautiful gifts for this little boy that we waited so anxiously to meet and the love that was showered upon us at this joyful time in our lives. Days like these cannot and will not ever be forgotten. I hope Philip knows how much he was loved even before we met him.

My due date was June 15, 2002. The week of Memorial Day, I went to work but had a doctor's appointment. I was retaining quite a bit of fluid, but I didn't realize it. My cousin Amy saw me the day or two before and said, "I don't like the way you look. When do you see the doctor?" She told me, "I think you'll probably stop working when he sees you." I left work early one day that week, and my supervisor said to me, "I don't think you're coming back." Well, they were all right. I went to my appointment, and he told me to stop working, "Go home, put your feet up, and you are to only be on your feet intermittently during the day." I stopped work a few weeks earlier than we had planned, but I didn't care. I had come this far with no problems and had no intentions to risk anything. I did nothing for three weeks. My wonderful mother-in-law did all my laundry, my mom cleaned my house and ironed all our clothes, and both mothers fed us for three weeks. I've got to say, it was pretty great! Well, June 15 came and went. Still no baby Philip. Then on the evening of June 17, I had no appetite. I remember saying to my husband that I didn't think I was going to make it to my next appointment a few days away. Within a few hours, my water broke and we left for the hospital. I went through the whole night with contractions, a pitocin drip, a nurse by my bedside, and my doctor monitoring my progress. The next afternoon, after an examination, I was not dilating. We made the decision to perform a C-Section. Within the hour on June 18, 2002, I gave birth by Cesarean Section to the cutest little redheaded boy I ever did see! Our gift from God had arrived. He made our life complete.

I miss my mother every day and there are some days I miss her more than others. My mom Carmelita was a wonderful human being. Everyone who knew her loved her. She had a dynamite personality and a brilliant smile that would lighten up the room when she was in it. She had a way with sayings that I must use in my daily dialogue at least once a week. "As Carmelita would say…" She and my dad had a dynamic that worked for them for fifty-nine years. I referred to them as Lucy and Ricky, from Lucille Ball and Desi Arnaz's show. She was the fun, energetic type and Dad was a musician just like Desi's character Ricky. She was family-oriented and each member held an important place in her heart. She was my very best friend. If I didn't see her every day, I talked to her at least more than once a day. I had preferred to be with her over any girlfriend I have had. I used to tell her, "Mom, you are my favorite person in this whole world." And I truly meant it.

Those closest to me often tell me that I'm so much like her, and I take that as a compliment. I was at work on a Saturday in January of 2011. I was working evenings at the time, three o'clock in the afternoon until eleven thirty in the evening. I had been working this shift since 2003 so I could have my mornings and early afternoons home with Philip. It was four o'clock that day when the call came. My cell phone rang and the caller identification was Mom's house phone. I had talked to her late morning when she came home from getting her hair done. She was making a pot of minestra soup. I reminded her that I was going to work and that I'd call her on my dinner time. This time, when I answered the phone, it wasn't Mom on the other end. It was her sister MaryLou. My stomach immediately turned. I knew instinctively something was not right. My aunt said, "Tina, honey, I think your mom is having a stroke." MaryLou was a retired registered nurse. She asked me which hospital I'd like her to tell the ambulance to take her to, where I worked in Scranton or to Wilkes-Barre where her family physician has privileges. I told her Wilkes-Barre. and I immediately left work to meet them there; it took me twenty-five minutes, but I beat the ambulance.

A lot happened in the emergency room before we were given a private room in the intensive care unit. All of my family came, her sisters, my cousins and their wives and husbands. It turned out to be a hemorrhagic bleed in her brain; nothing more could be done. I sat by her bedside holding her hand, her twin sister alongside me, caressing her arm and telling her that she can't leave her because they came into this world together and they're supposed to leave together. Her eyes never opened. It was heartbreaking. After what seemed like hours, Mom was moved into ICU. A few doctors came in to examine her, but all with the same conclusion. The hemorrhage in her brain was too much to perform surgery and even then it was a less than five percent chance of survival. Survival, not recovery. I leaned over and whispered in her ear, "I love you so much Mom." She managed to mumble a few words, "I know that." Those were the last words she spoke for the next five days until she passed. I slept in her room that night and the next. One afternoon a young nurse stepped in and told us they would be moving my mother to a private room on the fifth floor. My aunt Marylou, who stayed all day with me every day was there, still had a nurse's mentality and said, "So basically you need this room for another patient." And they did. I understood. Someone was probably assigned to that room following heart surgery, and since there was nothing more medically that could be done for mom, she had to be transferred upstairs. For the next few days, it was to be comfort measures for my mom.

I was not left alone any of those days. A family member was always with me. My cousin Tina Marie, who has a heart as big as

Manhattan and made of solid gold, slept with me as the snow fell outside and everything was covered in a white blanket. My husband would sit with me in the evenings, after helping Philip with his homework and making sure all his needs were met. Philip was only eight and a half years old. The staff were very obliging and made me as comfortable as possible. I talked to Mom when I'd have a few minutes alone. I know that even in a coma state, she heard me. I had just had a cholecystectomy a few weeks before and I was still not myself. I didn't feel good and I couldn't eat much, and I was struggling with my conscience if I was doing what I should be doing for her. My dad had passed away eighteen months prior and Mom was finally getting acclimated to a life without her partner. Every day I just looked at her. I wanted her to miraculously open her eyes and give me one more of those magnetic smiles of hers. It didn't happen. Every day I went over the years that we had each other, and I desperately tried to remember the sound of her voice and her laugh. I hope I never forget what she sounded like. I held her hand and stared at her long slender fingers. Her nails were always painted so nice. Her hair was always the same color; she never let herself go grey, even in her eighties, and went to a beauty salon every single week to have it done.

She was very active and went to the YMCA in Pittston every morning, Monday through Thursday. She swam with a group of lady friends and had them laughing even in the pool. She loved the water, and it kept her in good health for her age. She had virtually no ailments. My aunt and I reminisced about Mom as we sat together in that room. Our hearts grew heavier with each passing hour.

One evening, I was there all alone. My cousin Michael had just left and I was there in a peaceful hospital room, looking out the window at all the snow and thinking how beautiful it looked draped over the cars on the street and the tops of houses and buildings. Snow, really, is death. Everything in nature dies with snow. My mom was about to leave this earth and the life she knew. She was leaving all of us behind to be with her husband and parents again. This had to be better than lying in this hospital bed not able to move a muscle or open her eyes or smile. It was almost midnight, and I felt very weak. I got up to use the restroom and it felt like my legs were going to give out from under me as I walked. I can't explain why, but I made the decision to go home that night. Other than going home for a decent supper at my in-laws', I had not left the hospital that week. I blamed it on fatigue. I leaned over her bed and kissed her a few times on her forehead. I walked to the nurses' station and told them I had to leave, that I wasn't feeling well. They gave me a look of surprise, as if to say, after five days and now you're leaving? They probably knew the end was near. I came home and crawled into my bed. It was at least twelve-thirty in the morning. My home phone rang at four-thirty. My husband handed me the phone. It was her doctor. I already knew what he was going to say. And all I had to say when he told me she had just passed away was, "But I just left her."

Seven years later and I still think of those days, and I still wish I could pick up the phone to call her or get in my car and drive five minutes over the bridge to West Pittston to be with her. I suppose I will forever feel this way. Happy Mother's Day Carmie. I love you my best friend and confidante.

❦ ❦ ❦

Losing a parent is never easy, no matter the circumstances. It leaves you with an emptiness inside that never is filled again. My father had a few health problems, mostly heart, but he ate healthy and exercised when he was still able to. I somehow knew he would pass away before my mom. If it was the other way around, it would have been very difficult for him and for me. He relied on her for everything, as far as the house went. She did all the cleaning, cooking and laundry. She treated him like a king; she would say, "Who do you think you are Sam Maira, King Farouk?" King Farouk was the king of Egypt from 1936-1952, and he died in 1965 in Rome, Italy. As a kid I thought she made the name up just like all of her expressions. Losing my mom was a shock to me. I don't think I ever would have been ready to lose my best friend, even if she had been sick. Losing both parents within eighteen months felt like I had been orphaned. They were my connection to who I was, Sam and Carmelita's daughter. I will always be their daughter, but somehow it doesn't feel the same. I have trouble referring to myself in that manner because they are no longer here with me. They were essentially my identity. I had never attempted to find my birth parents, and now the two people who gave me a wonderful life are now gone. So much has happened in the past five years of my life, so much I needed to tell them and so many times I could have used my dad's advice...and I was alone. I thank God though that I have a great support system when I ask for it, with a tremendous family and intimate circle of friends. And my son, although only fifteen, is so kind and loving that I know I have him to lean on. We have each other.

I was living each day in a fog following my mom's death. I tried to be as present as I possibly could, but I had so much to take care of. I had to plan a funeral, clean out their home and put it up for sale, (something I think I did too quickly without much thought), and try to wrap my mind around what had just happened. If only I knew what the future held for me just two years later, I never would have sold the house. I would have lived in it with my son. My family was by my side through it all. My aunts became like moms to me and my cousins were my angels that offered love and support. My husband was there for me, but I needed him in a much bigger capacity. After a few months had passed, he stopped asking how I was coping. I blamed him and resented this, but I now realize that maybe he didn't know how to ask or didn't realize that I needed so much more compassion than he was already trying to offer to me. I think he felt that if I didn't ask for support, that I was ok. Well, I'm here to say, I wasn't. I suppose it was hard to know what to do or say when he still had his parents, but after so many years together, and him not realizing that I was so alone and hurting so much, it's sad. I know this was not intentional.

One day I realized that I needed professional help. I needed to go to a counselor to talk about my grief. It was grief that I had never experienced before and nothing or no one had the ability to help me. I made an appointment with a counselor, and after the first visit I knew I had done the right thing. I continued to see her for almost a year. I began my sessions after my aunt Lee (my mother's twin sister) had passed away five months after Mom. Losing my aunt was like losing my mother all over again. They were so identical, their voices, their hands, their loving ways and kindness. I used to joke when I was growing up, that I had two mothers.

Talking with Linda, my therapist, was a blessing. She made me realize over the course of this year that I had a few more issues going on within myself other than the loss of family. She asked me what I did for fun. I had no answer for her. I knew what I used to like to do, but I no longer did these things. Whether it was not making the time or perhaps loss of interest, either way I had no fun in my life. I suddenly realized I barely did anything for myself. My adult life was consumed with my

husband, my son, my parents and my in-laws. I guess that's how life

usually is, and it was admirable of me; however, I lost myself along the

way. We spent many many appointments talking about my sadness and

loss. And slowly the atmosphere changed and it led to discussions about

my unhappiness, my stifled voice, and the fact that I allow others to be

the directors in my life without any pushback. I never knew how to say

no. I'll never forget when she told me this, and I've used it to tell others

who I see struggling with the ability to stand up for themselves: "Every

time you say 'yes' to someone else, you are saying 'no' to yourself." For

example, a friend asks you to go see a movie, but in your mind you'd

much rather be under a blanket with a glass of wine enjoying the quiet

peacefulness of your home. You say yes and go because you don't want

to hurt your friend's feelings for fear they will get mad at you. Another

example, when it came to buying furniture or decorating our home, I

almost ninety-nine percent of the time allowed my ex-husband to make

all the decisions. I went along because I didn't have the courage to speak

up and say I didn't really care for that style. I allowed it to be this way for

all our married years. Good thing he had good taste, but that didn't mean it was my taste. It's almost like all my life, from teenager to adult, I went along with everyone else's decisions and opinions because I had a fear of being alienated from them. She taught me that I should be the first person to be taken care of, because if I'm not in a good emotional, mental, and physical shape, it will be impossible for me to care for my loved ones. Linda made me realize I had opinions and a voice, and I had every right to use it and to express myself. However, she warned me that, for those closest to me that were not used to me speaking up, it would be difficult for these individuals to adjust to this new attitude. This is exactly what happened. Not with my family. Not with my friends, which at the time there were very, very few. But it was true of my ex-husband. He did not like this at all. I remember him saying to me on the phone one day, after we had separated, that if this was my new way of communicating, he didn't like it. I was coined as being aggressive. *Well, too damn bad,* I thought. I was communicating better than I ever had but it wasn't his way of communicating. I've since learned to be much more tactful when I speak, but if you ask me my opinion, be prepared. I will be honest but not hurtful.

Meeting with Linda on a weekly basis helped me to look at my life situation differently. I slowly began to think about myself without jeopardizing my commitment to my family. I learned to say no, but say it diplomatically as not to push my loved ones away. My aunts and my cousins were very proud of me, telling me that finally I am becoming who they knew was buried deep inside this body. They admired me for this. Towards the end of our year, the subject of my marriage came to the surface. More tears and more anxiety. She and I both knew that the marriage was in trouble, and we needed counseling, but these issues did not, in my heart, warrant divorce. I truly believe they could have been dealt with and the relationship could have been saved. But by the time we tried to work on our issues, it was too late, or perhaps we didn't work hard enough. I thank Linda all the time in my mind for the help she gave me and it was because of this positive experience that I would recommend therapy to everyone.

It's been seven years since Mom passed away. I think about her every day. I miss her every day. I know she is doing fine up there; she's with her twinnie and they are happy. Their two hearts are joined again. And I know she and my dad are with me every day. They know what I have faced, and I have no doubt they know things will work out for me. Their spirits were probably what gave me the strength that I never knew I had to forge ahead and to begin to live my life the way I want to. No doubt I still feel stress and anxiety from day to day, but I have to take a really deep breath and reassure myself that I have the tools necessary to cope and to make intelligent decisions about my life and my future. It's definitely not easy, but easier, knowing I'm in control.

I haven't talked about my family too much thus far. It would be an injustice if I didn't. I was raised in a very tight-knit Italian family, on both parent's sides. The type of family that got together just for the hell of it, not just on holidays and birthdays or funerals. We spent time together during the week or on a weekend. And we all knew what was happening in each other's lives. Good or bad, that's the way it was. There was harmony. We genuinely enjoyed each other's company and looked forward to being together. And in a time of need, you always knew they were there to help and be a support. There was love. I know that I can rely on my aunts and my uncle and especially my cousins -- each one of them -- for anything. My cousins are the brothers and sisters that I never had. I know they feel the same way about me. For a time after Mom passed, it just slipped out and I addressed my Aunt MaryLou as "Mom." I guess because I probably talked to my mother more than anyone else in my life and it comes out naturally. One day when it happened, I had tears in my eyes and she kindly said to me, "It's okay, I'm honored you called me that." I cry a lot, but it's better than holding emotions inside until you make yourself sick. I used to do that, but not anymore. We are all busy, and sometimes making extra time to visit with my family is difficult. I'm working full-time now since my divorce, and my free time is precious to me. My cousins and I try to keep in touch and some I talk to or text at least once a week. But if that's not possible, we still know we are there for each other. My cousin MaryEllen has lived abroad for the past twenty-eight years or so. She comes home to Pittston a few times a year to spend a few weeks with her mom, my mother's sister Sara. After Mom died, MaryEllen made it a point to call me once a week without fail. She was living in Manila, then Brazil and now Ecuador -- and still we talk once a week. She has talked me through my grief after my mom and through my heartache of my divorce.

All of my cousins were there for me when I needed them the most. I don't mean to single out anyone, because honestly, I don't know what I would do without them. Each one means the world to me and I love them with all the love in my heart. Tommy, Mary Ellen, Michael, Louis, Jimmy, Tammy, Amy, Charlie and Tina Marie. Their spouses all hold a special place in my heart too, Sheila, Ernst, Maureen, Gloria, Donna, Andy, Mike, Susan and Joe. We are so fortunate to have each other and to have each other close by. We've never exchanged harsh words or never had a rift between any of us. How unusual is that! Very often I hear of families that don't speak or have an ongoing animosity that started with their parents and it becomes a lifestyle. Not my family. I never could quite understand such things because this was never the way my family was or is to this day. Again, harmony and love are two very important key elements in a family, or even in friendships. Trust is big, too. Without trust there is nothing. I could honestly say without a doubt that I trust each of my cousins with my life. I'm sure not a lot of people could admit that, but I could. These are hardworking, honest, respectful, intelligent, loyal individuals who would give you the proverbial shirt off their back. I am genuinely proud they are my family. I was brought into this family as a stranger at three and a half months old, and instantly I was one of them. I am immensely grateful for the love they give me and I couldn't imagine my life without them.

❦ ❦ ❦

It's funny how there are certain things and people that become a constant in our lives. We go through the years always expecting them to be there and be a part of our everyday life. I was so fortunate to have my parents until I was in my late forties. I was forty-six when my dad passed away in 2009 and forty-eight when Mom passed in 2011. They watched me grow up, graduate high school and college, get married, and become a mom. Short-lived were the years Dad got to watch my son grow; Philip was only seven when he passed. But they were quality years; I was working only part time second shift and I made sure my parents spent time with him few times a week, whether it was walking together in the cemetery behind their house, Philip riding his tricycle there because it was nice and flat and had few cars, or even filling up the little plastic pool in their backyard so my mom and I could sit in it with Philip. I wanted to make sure my son knew my parents and my in-laws in order for him to not forget them. My parents were quite a few years older than my in-laws, and I was making memories for him. When he was little, I'd lay in bed with him until he was ready to fall asleep and once in a while he'd ask me to tell him a story about my life -- be careful what you wish for, Philip, because now you're getting an entire book! I had many stories to tell. I told him stories about my grandparents, and how I loved spending time with them. I told him about family vacations with my cousins at the Jersey Shore. I told him how my grandmother Tina took myself and my cousin Tina Marie to California for two weeks to visit her cousins when I was thirteen, and my cousin got a terrible sunburn. That wasn't fun, but what was fun was the fact that three Tina Maira's were sitting in a row on the airplane! Of course I had to tell these stories with excitement and an inflated tone of voice so it would be dramatic. He got a kick out of it. Looking intently at me with that flaming red hair and eyes so dark brown like olives, certainly times like those cannot be replaced and will never be forgotten. I told him about when my family would all go to this cabin at Lake Wallenpaupack that was a conference center for a company one of my uncles, Tom (Uncle Skippy) Murtha, worked for. We slept in bunk beds, and the living space had an enormous stone fireplace. No tv; no stereo; the only phone was a pay phone on the wall. It was set on a lake, about an hour from home. We were there three times on different occasions for the weekend. I told him of the silly shenanigans my cousins would take part in on those weekends. He would giggle and think it was so funny, and it was. Even to this day, when we are alone travelling on vacation or quietly at home with each other, I continue to tell him all about my family and my life. I know he appreciates it. I recently told him that he had to promise me, if anything happens to me (now I sound like Carmelita, she always prefaced with that when she was about to tell me something important), he is never ever to throw out or give away any of my photo albums or my mom's for that matter. I told him to promise me he will put them all in a safe place, wherever that may be when he's grown and has moved away, and to cherish them forever.

It's our entire life captured within Kodak film. Her photos survived Hurricane Agnes Flood in 1972, and they are all I cared about when I emptied my parents home. I continue to look at them all the time, and I continue to take thousands of pictures too, so that someday when I leave this earth, my son will have decades of moments to cherish.

❧ ❧ ❧

Don't be like Gatsby. A few days ago, I had a serious conversation with my son while driving in the car. I seem to always start by saying, "I'm just going to give you some sound advice, it's up to you if you take it or not. I'm not lecturing, but I just want to give you some insight." I had reflected upon a recent conversation I had with someone, and that someone was boasting about an expensive purchase she had made, because she "had" to. I thought about that conversation that night and the symbolism behind it. Without mentioning any names or explaining why I wanted to discuss this with him, I began. I told him my best advice going forward is to always be yourself. He attends a college preparatory school and interacts with students from all over the world, twenty-one countries in fact. He'll be going away to college, so this advice will serve him well. I told him to never ever feel he has to put on airs to impress people. "Don't be someone that you are not, because once you do, it's like a snowball rolling down a steep hill; it becomes a way of life and you are in a constant state of pretending. You lose sight of who you really are." I think it's true for some people, and for this woman I was conversing with, it's due to insecurity and the need for a constant form of affirmation from friends, family, and strangers. They crave it, and without it they are miserable and depressed and eventually will take this out on those around them that care for them the most. I told him that outsiders will see through this facade and realize this, because people are smarter than we want to give them credit for. I told him no one wants to be around this type of person and slowly they will become a loner. I believe people want to surround themselves with others that are genuine, honest, down to earth, good people. No one likes a phony or a want-to-be. Just be yourself -- the best advice I could give him. Oftentimes those who are pretentious will come across as condescending, sarcastic, or just simply rude. Ironically, if you are living your life always feeling you have to have the best of everything...clothes, cars, jewelry, designer handbags...you'll find that you're not happy and never are you going to be satisfied. I ended the conversation by telling him, "Don't be like Gatsby." He laughed and said, "I KNEW you were going to say that!" He had just read this exemplary novel by the great American writer, F. Scott Fitzgerald, in his last trimester in school, so I knew he would be able to relate. For those of you who have not read this book, I highly recommend you do. It's a rather short paperback full of symbolism and life lessons. Gatsby lived a life of pretending and exuded a vulgar display of wealth. He did not come from old money, but, rather new money, nouveau riche, and he had set his life out to impress Daisy, who had been born into generations of wealth. He threw lavish parties at his mansion with hundreds of people who had never met him, only in the hopes that she would hear about these parties that were being held across the water from where she lived, and that she would attend and he would finally get to see her again. He did not attend his own parties; he had no desire to meet any of these strangers who were there only to be seen and to say that they had been to Gatsby's mansion; he was using them and they were using him. Long story short, there are a number of twists as the story unravels, loaded with deception and fakeness. It doesn't end well, for any one. As I listened to this person, her story had only one truth to it as I could see it. She had been in the company of a stranger, and nonchalantly making this pricey purchase in front of them was only to give the impression that she could. I know better than this stranger. Unfortunately, this person does not even realize this herself, she doesn't know any other way to be. Don't be like Gatsby.

My son turned sixteen two weeks ago. All of a sudden I feel like he's a man and not just my boy. I am so immensely proud of him. He's mature beyond his years and I could see that with every passing day, he is appreciating everything I do for him. He tells me he loves me every day and always asks how I'm doing, "How are you Mom, everything ok? You feel good?" I tell him yes, most of the time, but I also confide in him when I'm not feeling so good. He understands, and I know he cares about my well being. He's always asking what he can do for me, or if I need anything. This is something fairly new, and I think it's because he's starting to realize that he is the most important person in my life, and I would do anything to provide him

with what he needs, emotionally, physically, and mentally. We have many private conversations and I value his opinion and I know he values mine.

He got his driver's permit the day after his birthday. His dad and I have taken him driving around our local school's parking lot and soon he'll be taking lessons from a driving academy. His freedom will expand and his dependence on me and his dad will lessen in the days to come. This is hard. Not unusual or unnatural, but it's hard. I took him out on the local streets and neighborhoods the last two days and let me tell you, it's not so easy being in the passenger seat and putting your confidence in a sixteen-year-old behind the wheel for the first time.

Thirty-eight years ago, someone had the same confidence in me. My cousin Louis had the courage to teach me to drive. He took me to the parking lot around Pittston Area High School, so that's where I began with Philip. Louis must have been very patient because, number one, I was a teenage girl, and number two, I had to learn to drive with my dad's car that was at least two blocks long, and there was no back-up camera! But, I did it and so will my son. He's cautious and says he's not nervous at all. Well, good for him. As I sit in that passenger's seat, I look over at him, and all I see in front of me is this beautiful little redhead sitting in a carseat in the back seat of my car, singing along to songs on the Disney Radio. How could it be possible that now he's driving me around? He is also going to a tutor for SAT prep. College is only two years away -- if I feel melancholy now, I hate to think what I'll feel in 2020. I didn't go away to college; I stayed local in Scranton, PA. Philip has made it clear he will be going away to college. Ironically, because I didn't go away I always said to others that everyone should do at least one of these three things: go away to college, live on your own before getting married, and live with the person you're marrying before marrying them. I did none of these things, but I still believe it's a good idea. One should live alone and learn to take care of themselves and a house or apartment whatever it may be, to cook and clean and support themselves, before having to do it for themselves and a spouse. I didn't do this simply because I didn't know any better. This is the summer of Philip. He's learning to drive; I'm teaching him to cook; I've been taking him to the bank with me and teaching him how to make a deposit and cash a check. He's also making more plans with his friends from school and is enjoying a social life. All part of growing up.

Carmela (Nellie) Baiera Tuttilmond. My grandmother, on Mom's side -- what a wonderful woman. The oldest of eight children, she was married at the age of sixteen. She married Louis Biscotto Tuttilmond. Papa was a few years older than Grandma. They lived at 28 West Oak Street in Pittston in a darling little house with a front porch and back porch and a sweet backyard with a white bird bath in the middle with flowers on the ground all around it. It was painted light blue in the bowl so that the water looked like Caribbean waters. Every year my grandmother scraped it with a wire brush to remove the peeling chips of paint to repaint it so it looked nice for the summer. She loved rose bushes and peonies, which lined the perimeter of the yard. My grandfather passed away in 1972 and my grandmother in 1992, and that was the last time I was in that little house, yet I can vividly recall every square inch of it. After Papa died, she lived there until her passing. It was there they lived their lives and raised their family. My grandparents had a baby girl, first born and her name was Carmelina. She passed away at fifteen or sixteen months old of pneumonia. Not long after, the twins were born, my mom Carmelita and her twin Leona, on June 2 of 1928. My great-grandmother Nona delivered the twins at home. In 1928 there were no ultrasounds, and after the delivery of my mom, Nona was just as shocked as my grandmother that there was another baby inside. Twin baby girls, inseparable forever. Three years later, in 1931, Sara was born and ten years after Sara, in 1941 Mary Louise was born. Poor Papa in a house of all women! Poor Grandma being married at sixteen!

It was in this house on West Oak Street in Pittston that our family shared so many memories. If I had to paint a virtual tour in my mind of that house that held for me and all of my family so many wonderful times, it would be this: Walking through the front door into the living room; a couch, an easy chair with an ottoman, and a recliner in the opposite corner; a sofa table under the front window facing the front porch and the street, with a lamp in the middle. I can picture Papa sitting in that easy chair, always with dress pants and a white collared dress shirt on -- sometimes suspenders -- and the top few buttons unbuttoned on his shirt. He loved television; his favorite shows were *Manix* (a detective story) and *Bonanza* (a western about a father raising three sons on a ponderosa).

Walking through the living room took you to the dining room. It was in this dining room that Christmas Eve dinner was enjoyed every year, with the adults at the big table and us grandchildren, eight of us, eating at the kitchen table. We didn't even care that we were in there and not with the adults, because that's where all the fun was and where the shenanigans happened. Christmas dinner was baked spaghetti or homemade manicotti. My grandmother made her own manicotti and her own cannolis. However, being young and our gourmet palates not yet developed, we never cared for peas in our baked spaghetti (I suppose this was her version of pasta bolognese), so the battle of the peas began. Not quite sure which one of us started it, but I'm pretty sure it was either Louis or Michael the throwing of one pea into another's soda glass was all it would take! After dinner, we enjoyed grandma's cannolis. It seemed it was always Mary Ellen's job to fill the cannolis with homemade cream (hm, I wonder why). It's very easy to fill and taste! That cream was so delicious; I have yet to taste one as good as hers. When all the dishes were cleaned up, the best part of Christmas Eve happened, the exchanging of gifts. My grandparents and later just Grandma, bought for all of us. Everyone else received gifts from their godparents. If all of us girls got velour robes from Vanity Fair (those robes were like iron!), we knew someone went to Reading to the Vanity Fair outlet, and Grandma gave them money to buy four robes for her four granddaughters. We always had a good laugh at that one. So, dinner and dessert was over, bellies were full, gifts exchanged and a total mess of wrapping paper in the living room -- on the floor, on the couch, at our feet. So began the annual paper fight. We rolled it up in balls and threw it at each other, laughing until our stomachs hurt and tears rolled down our cheeks. We caught someone off guard and laughed at the look on their face. It may sound so simple and so silly, but we did it every year, we knew it was coming, yet we laughed and laughed about it every time.

Continuing on the tour, through the dining room was the kitchen. This is what I remember most about the kitchen. There was a small niche with a built-in desk where I did plenty of homework when Mom picked me up from school and we went right to my grandmothers for supper. My father worked late two nights a week, getting home after 9:00 pm, so

Mom and I usually ate supper at my grandparents. Sometimes it was just the four of us; sometimes more, maybe one of my aunts and uncles joined us. There was a drawer in that desk with all kinds of neat things. All of my cousins probably did homework at that desk at one time or another, and often it was the catch all drawer for our stuff. There was a portable tv in the corner on the counter. Every night we watched *Dialing For Dollars*, wondering who would win when the host spun the wheel around. Next to the tv was a white rectangular transistor radio -- an AM radio! I picture my grandfather leaning on his elbows to hear better (he wore a hearing aid in his older years), with a pen and a piece of scrap paper. Every day he jotted down the day's Dow Jones Industrial, taking notes on his stock. When I think about this, I'm pretty impressed. A man of no formal education, coming here from Italy as a young man, and he knew enough to invest in the stock market. Grandma kept track of that stock long after he passed away and dealt with her broker for many years.

There was a staircase in the dining room that led to the second floor, which had three bedrooms and a bathroom. The twins shared a room in the back of the house, Sara and Marylou were in the bedroom in the middle, and my grandparents were in the front of the house. The bathroom was completely tiled with light blue tile -- floor, walls and ceiling. It had a revolving toothbrush holder in the wall above the sink. I thought that was so cool. My grandparents had a white bedroom suite. After my grandmother died, I was given the bedroom furniture. I kept it in my second bedroom for many years. When my son was old enough for a big bed, we reassembled it. I, like my grandmother, believed paint could do miracles and make something old new again. I sanded all the pieces and painted it navy blue. We bought new beddings and voila! Philip had his new bedroom suite. He used that furniture until 2011. It must have been around 90 years old.

Looking through my mom's photos, I see my first birthday being celebrated in my grandparents house -- me in a highchair at the head of her dining room table, surrounded by my grandparents and my grandmother Tina Maira. All of my aunts and uncles and my cousins are posing for pictures around me. My first Christmas with my adopted family was in December 1964 and was celebrated in that home on West Oak Street. My mom was recuperating from surgery, so we stayed there.

I took my first steps in that house, and Grandma bought me my first doll stroller with a baby doll in the seat. I have an adorable picture of that: "My first Christmas with my family." Those are very powerful words for me. I was born December 11,1963, two weeks before Christmas. I wasn't adopted until March 26, 1964. I don't even know where I was or who was taking care of me for my first Christmas in 1963. Mom always told me that it was a woman who was taking care of me, but I have no idea who she was, or if that's even true. I'm not even sure she knew. Whatever information I have about my life those first three and a half months does not tell me who took care of me until my biological parents relinquished their rights. For all I know, I could've still been with Marilyn. Well, after 1964, I can say I have had wonderful Christmases every single year of my life!

❦ ❦ ❦

We had a tradition in Pittston, where the part of Italy your family came from would be celebrated in Church. They held a special Mass on Sunday and a big procession with the priest, the altar boys, and members of the Church societies and the community. Our family was from Serradifalco, Sicily. Our holiday was September 18, or around that date if it was on a Sunday. It was the feast of Our Lady of Sorrows. There is a statue dedicated for this procession, and the members of the Serradifalco Society (the men of course) would carry this statue during the procession, all through the streets of Pittston. They made many stops along the way for people to pin dollars to her dress, and for the men to have a glass of wine or a shot of whiskey at their friends' houses along the journey. I can't tell you how many of these processions I walked with my mom and aunts. It was very special to my grandmother; after mass all of us would have dinner at her house, with homemade manicotti and all the sides -- meatballs, chicken, salad and wine. It was such a big deal that every year her cousins would travel here from Brooklyn and stay for three or four days just for the feast day. It was an all-day affair. Mass at 11:00, dinner at 12:30, and walk the procession at 3:00. We didn't leave that house the entire day; it was just like any other holiday for our family. After she was gone, I walked it a few times. Then after that, I just went to the Mass and waited outside with the parishioners until the men of the parish took the statue of the Blessed Mother outside to prepare for the procession. That church, the church my parents were married in and both my son, his dad, and I were baptized in, has since closed. Another wonderful tradition is gone, but the memories of those glorious days full of love and family and togetherness will never go away.

I've been thinking about people and their communication skills, or lack thereof. I've come across individuals in my life that truly believe they are great communicators, but in fact they are horrible at it. You are either born with it or perhaps it can be learned, but not without first realizing that your approach and presentation are what communication is all about. Tact and tone has so much to do with it and even body language plays a significant part. I think it may be a sign of the times, everyone is on high alert and we tend to react instead of respond. I used to be guilty of being a reactor…I cry very easily and I can get hurt very easily. I will be the first to admit that I am an emotional person. I no longer believe that part of me is a bad thing. If that's how I react to someone who is nasty or condescending to me, well, at least they know how I feel, no hiding how what was said affected me. It's not silly, it's not immature, and it's not abnormal.

I have a difficult time understanding people whose first instinct is to belittle someone with a differing opinion or the way I handle a situation may not necessarily be the way they would handle it. And now, in a world of texting and emailing, it makes it difficult to interpret emotions with text. Text messages cause so many misunderstandings. We feel the need to overuse capital letters and punctuation to get our point across, which hurts feelings and leads to people getting upset or even mad and disgusted. Where did we lose the courage to pick up the telephone and actually have a mature conversation? Our first response is often that it is a sign of the times; we live in a world of technology. I have nothing against technology, but it takes away our ability to have intelligent and meaningful conversations with those we love. Maybe we find texting easier because we otherwise would not have the courage to say things to our friends. Again, it all comes down to how we approach a subject and our tone. Believe it or not, you can get your point across without hurting the other person's feelings.

Again, it's all about communication skills. Friendships and relationships fall apart due to bad communication. There's a saying that my cousin Amy told me once, and I have seen it quoted several times since, "Tact is the ability to tell someone to go to hell, and they look forward to the trip." Enough said.

Divorce is a life-altering event. I'm sure in some cases it's for the better and perhaps a life saving event in a volatile marriage. However, when it comes upon you unexpectedly, it's a death. It becomes a time of anger, sadness, and mourning. And sometimes even after all is said and done, every once in a while these emotions resurface. Reliving the divorce can take control of your emotions and affect you for a brief moment in time. I don't believe what some people say, that when it's over, it's over. Oh sure, the marriage is over. Sharing a home and a life together is certainly over. But the longer your marriage was, the more detailed history you have shared, makes moving on that more difficult. Like my therapist once said, "No one goes to that altar and says to themselves, 'I'll give it ten years and we'll see how it goes from there.'" We fall in love with whom we believe is "the one," we date for what we believe is a sufficient amount of time to get to know each other, and then when the time is right, we start the planning.

I knew Al was the one I wanted to spend my life with. We planned the engagement, we planned the wedding, and we basically planned our lives. We decided what kind of engagement ring to buy, we picked out invitations, we decided on a venue for the big event, we found a place to live to begin our life together, and so on and so on. I'm pretty sure no one plans on when to get divorced. I know I never planned on it, never in my wildest dreams. We had a good foundation, I thought, and I always believed that no marriage or relationship is perfect; it always takes effort, and there is no issue not worth fighting for when you love your partner. Even when there seemed to be issues in our marriage, the thought of divorce wasn't part of the bigger scheme of my life. We made a commitment, we exchanged vows, and with our dearest families and closest friends present, we were bestowed a blessing to live a happy life together. Reality? Maybe for some, about fifty percent. Perhaps at the present day, that percentage may be less. Three close friends and I recently got on this subject. As couples grow and mature together, we change a little every year. We are who we are. When one partner changes so drastically that you no longer have anything in common or anything to talk about except matters concerning the children or our job or even the family pet, there is a serious problem. Of course it's understandable when we are in the midst of raising our children; sometimes couples lose sight of the fact they are spending less and less time together as adults and doing adult things. What's even more disheartening is when one partner sees this and realizes this but the other does not. I'm going out on a limb here by what I'm about to say, but I'm here to say it anyway. I think because of a woman's natural intuition, she may realize that her marriage is in trouble but the husband does not. Females and males are wired differently. It's a fact. There have been symposiums on this matter, and scientific studies have proven that men and women are chemically different and we are "wired" differently. The big problem is when one tries to tell the other that they see a problem arising and the other denies it and or makes excuses for the behavior. Before you know it, the distance between husband and wife becomes so wide, it's damaged beyond repair. I have a friend who is a priest and when I was going through my divorce, I spoke to Paul at great length from time to time, for support, and comfort and maybe some advice that I couldn't get from a family member. Surprisingly, he told me that I'd be surprised how two people can be going down this road of life and all it takes is one to take a turn off a side road and the two never meet at the end. He did not try to convince me that it would be sinful if this ended in divorce, but that if I've done all I could with my heart, then everything would be ok. As a woman, I saw the changes happening right in front of me. We didn't change together or grow together. I was left out of my husband's changing life. I didn't care very much for his new personality, ideas, and beliefs. It was foreign to me, and it was changing the course of our life together, and he didn't seem to care. I was left guessing all the time. *Where was this change coming from? What influence in his life was changing our course and determining our fate?* When someone changes too quickly and so drastically, it's very hard to understand.

I have taken a break from writing over the past six weeks or so. Not because I haven't wanted to but I was guilty of what I say never to do. I let my free time be occupied with things that could probably always wait to be taken care of, but I felt compelled to do them. I must get back on track and reserve time for my writing. It's helpful to me to express my thoughts and life experiences by putting these thoughts into words and stories on a blank piece of paper.

I was away for two weeks with my son on a vacation which we referred to as "a trip of a lifetime." And it actually was. This was the first time my son left the country, and he hadn't been on an airplane in many years. We traveled to Ecuador to vacation with my cousin, her husband, and their three sons. We had been planning this trip since last September and it went off without any problems. Her husband had told me, "Just get yourself and Philip here, and we will take care of you." It was marvelous. We traveled to other cities, experienced things for the first time that I nor my son would have ever thought to do, and I even tried new foods...which if you knew me is really out of my comfort zone. Every day spent there made me realize how very blessed I am. Not because I was able to plan this trip with Philip, but because I know beyond a shadow of a doubt that I have people in my life that love us, care about us, and want to show their support. I knew this all along; however, this trip left an everlasting impression on me and my son and made me realize that no matter how tough life gets and no matter how many bumps may lay in the road of life, there is always hope. There are always people out there who want to show that love and make you realize that everything will be okay -- friends and family alike; in this case it was family. The generosity and love I felt those two weeks will be burned in my memory for a lifetime. And because I'm Carmelita's daughter, I took hundreds of pictures because I didn't want to miss capturing these memories on film. I look at most of them on a daily basis, and I can't help but smile and say to myself, "Damn, I'm a lucky woman." I did not worry about a thing, I did not stress over anything, and I did not even give a thought as to whether this was the right trip at the right time in our lives. It was perfect, the best quality family time I could've given to Philip. He thanked me numerous times and told me never ever in his wildest dreams did he think that this is what this trip was going to entail. He didn't ask for souvenirs even though I encouraged it. He told me that the photos and the memories were enough for him. This is only the first of many trips I will make with him -- at least until he doesn't want to go with his mom anymore. I owe a super thank you to MaryEllen and Ernst and their sons, Ernst, Samuel and Thomas, for allowing Philip and I to join in on their family time and for making a lasting impression on my son and myself, proving once again that I have been so fortunate to be a part of this wonderful family of mine, whose willingness to give love and support is infinite.

Dad. Sam Carmen (Salvatore) Maira. Born on March 26, 1925, in Pittston, Pennsylvania to two Italian immigrants from Sicily. He was fair-skinned, with crystal blue eyes and blonde wavy hair. He attended public school and lived in Pittston until he and my mom moved to West Pittston after they were married a few years. Dad was a man of old-fashioned ideals, and these ideals paved the path on which he raised me. He taught me respect, he taught me how to be self sufficient, and he encouraged me to always do well in school. And because I am who I am, I did all that was within my power to make him proud. I feel I was a good daughter. I never embarrassed him, I was never disrespectful, and I handled myself with poise and grace in public. I grew up always doing the right thing and there were things I'd never do for fear that he would "kill me" -- of course I only mean that figuratively, but my fear was that I would make him mad, and I only wanted harmony in our house; it was rare that there wasn't. He was very vocal when it came to giving me his opinion on the company I kept, no holding back there. If he didn't like a certain boy coming to the house, or if he didn't like the parents of a boy, well, he let me know about it. I used to think he was so mean when he did that. I realize now that he was looking out for my best interest like any good parent would; maybe he felt he had better intuition than I, and he was probably right. Every family has days when parents argue, siblings fight, or parents scream at their children. I don't remember there being too much of that in our home growing up. However, being raised in this fashion also meant I never stood up for myself. It probably wasn't until I was a college student that my dad and I would have adult conversations about life, politics, religion, business, people, etc. I think at that point he must have realized that I wasn't a child anymore.

Our quality father-daughter times were the two or three trips a year to Manhattan. We did plenty of talking for those few hours in the car, and I think he looked forward to doing that with me. We never left New York without a taxi ride to Little Italy where we'd have an early dinner on Mulberry Street and take fresh Italian bread and salami home from a deli he liked on Mott Street. Most of the time that salami was eaten before we got to the Delaware Water Gap...we'd just just roll it up and eat it or tear off some bread and eat it that way. When he felt I was ready to handle Manhattan traffic, we would switch driving around Hackettstown, New Jersey and he'd let me "take it in." He taught me how to maneuver around those congested streets of Midtown with the forever-impatient New York drivers. Eventually, it got to the point where I did all the driving. I appreciate him allowing me to do that because I feel comfortable driving to New York to this day. I've made the trip to the city many times with my son, and while we're walking the streets, I feel compelled to tell him about those times with his grandfather. I'm sure I tell him the same stories every time but he never says, "you're repeating yourself, Mom." He just listens with a smile and knows I tell these stories to keep my memories of Dad alive.

When I got married, I remained in West Pittston for five years, and then we bought a home in Pittston. We never discussed moving out of town, and I can't say if it was even a thought. I'm sure if it had been because of a job we would've considered it. I sort of felt that I also had the responsibility of taking care of my parents, especially as they aged. They only had me. Of course they had siblings and nieces and nephews, but a child just knows best when it comes to looking after aging parents. I was very fortunate that Mom and Dad were healthy individuals and really enjoyed their independent life. They spent the winters in Florida, so they certainly didn't need me then! Dad had a few health problems, cardiac mostly. He had a quadruple bypass in 2000 and a year later surgery to repair an abdominal aortic aneurysm. This was a mild setback for him but he was stubborn and determined. He didn't even agree to go to cardiac rehabilitation here in Wilkes-Barre. His rehab was to be walking the beach everyday with Mom in Florida, and that's exactly what he did.

Dad was seventy-five years old when he had quadruple bypass surgery, and he and Mom were going to be celebrating their 50th wedding anniversary. They were married on December 27, 1950. A big party was already in the planning stages and invitations were sent out to one hundred people or so. We regrouped our strategy and decided to postpone the celebration until the surgery was over. The surgery went well and so did his recovery. The bypass surgery gave him another ten years with us, and he lived those ten years as he had lived all of his years, spending the winters in Florida, enjoying his family and friends, and welcoming his one and only grandchild in 2002. Following his recovery, we celebrated their 50th wedding anniversary with a gathering of all their friends and family. Dad was doing great and as always, he thoroughly enjoyed the occasion. In the years to follow, another surgery was necessary, for an abdominal aortic aneurysm, but he recovered from that too and made a few more trips to Florida.

One early Saturday morning in April of 2009, my house phone rang. Mom told me that Dad had fallen and she thought maybe he broke a hip. Only eighteen months prior, they had purchased a one level townhouse a few streets over from our family home. The house on York Avenue was big and was beginning to be too much work for them, even though I helped Mom with the cleaning, and I did the yardwork. I understood their concerns, and although it didn't settle right with me to give up the only home I knew, I knew it was a necessary evil. Even though this new home was manageable and without stairs to climb, accidents will still happen. I hung up the phone, called work to use a sick day, and drove over the bridge to West Pittston. I wasn't sure what I would find when I got there, but right behind me was the ambulance. Dad was lying on the floor not moving. He was coherent and didn't seem to be in any noticeable pain. He couldn't move, which is probably best if he had broken his hip. He was assessed by the paramedics and transported to the hospital. It was here that x-rays showed a broken hip and broken shoulder on the same side. The broken hip turned out to be a broken femur, but towards the upper part. He had another surgery to put a rod in the femur and the shoulder was immobilized. Two or three days later, the social worker from the hospital informed us he would be moved to a skilled nursing facility for rehabilitation for the hip. It was a very long road for Dad. He could not bear weight on the leg for a few weeks, and he couldn't use a walker due to the broken shoulder on the same side.

This was my first time ever seeing my dad in a wheelchair and in a nursing home. Ironically, it was the same nursing home where I had been a nurses' aide during my college years and where his mom was for five years prior to her death. A lot had changed in that facility, and I was very impressed with the care and the physical therapy he received. Mom went to see him every day, bringing him his favorite foods and desserts…just doing what she always had done for him all of these years. I also went at least three days a week, while Philip was in school, and we would visit on the weekends. The facility is operated by Methodist Homes and only ten minutes from our house, very convenient for Mom. Dad's fall was in the middle of April and he did not come home until the week of Father's Day, in June. I arranged for therapy at their house and a visiting nurse came one or two times a week to assess him and take vital signs. I had to help him shower, and that in itself was a hurdle for him. I suppose it's never easy for a grown, proper man to have a female help him, nevertheless a daughter. It was upsetting for him at first, and with tears in his eyes, he called me his angel but told me how embarrassed he was and that he never wanted me to have to do this for him. I told him firmly but with love, "Dad, I am a grown woman; I was a nurses' aide for six years. I'm a wife and a mother...I've seen it all. So get over it Sam Maira, because I'm all you've got." He cried and said ok, and that was that.

My father was only home for two weeks before returning to the hospital. One evening at the end of June, I got a call from my cousin MaryEllen. She was home in Pittston visiting with one of her sons, and she was at my parents' house with her mom, my Aunt Sara. My father was in bad shape. MaryEllen is also a registered nurse, and she believed he was in congestive heart failure. She called the ambulance, and I raced over there. He looked awful. His face and his lips were twice the size they should have been. He could hardly breathe, he kept his eyes closed, and he couldn't really speak to us. My mom went with him in the ambulance and I followed in my car. This time, his stay in the hospital would be the last. He remained in the hospital for weeks, eventually refusing therapy and refusing to eat. He was becoming very thin and his voice was weak. I knew what was happening, and I tried to gently tell Mom, too. She stayed with us a few nights every week and a few nights with her twin sister. I didn't want her to be alone, and I had informed the hospital that I was to be the point of contact, not Mom. The decision was made to move Dad to hospice on July 23. I had told his family physician, who is also my physician, that I did not want my father to have any pain, and I wanted all the comfort measures possible. He obliged and made the arrangements. The day before the transfer, I sat on the side of his bed, and I really tried to explain to him what was going to happen. I told him he had to be transferred to another facility where it would be quiet and he would be comfortable. I made sure he knew it wasn't a nursing home, because as weak as he was he let it be known he was not to go to a nursing home. The next morning I went to hospice before he arrived to do the paperwork. As I was sitting at a table with the director, my dad was wheeled in by the ambulance crew. I got up and gave him a kiss on the cheek and said, "Good morning Dad." He was more alert that day than he had been in two weeks; he looked at me with those crystal blue eyes, so terribly skinny and small on the gurney, reminding me so much of his dad, my grandfather Joe Maira. He said to me, "Do you have any more surprises for me?" He knew where he was. I was sick to my stomach. The nurses followed him to his room and transferred him into the bed and made him comfortable. After the paperwork was done, I went to his room to face him. He was very quiet and didn't say too much. I tried to explain to him all that I possibly could. He reached out to hold my hand and said "I guess this is the end." We both cried. I assured him the nurses would make him comfortable and make sure he didn't experience any pain. This was on a Thursday. I went with my mom every day, often leaving for work from there (I had been working evening shift at that time), and someone would pick my mom up at night. Sunday, Mom and I went to visit Dad and I left to go to work. Mom stayed, and my cousin Jimmy was there to visit him and keep Mom company. After he left, my cousin's son Joseph gave Mom a ride to her sister Leona's. At six o'clock that evening, I received a call at work. I answered the phone in my department of the laboratory, and when the woman identified herself, I knew immediately what she was about to say. Dad had passed away ten minutes earlier. I called my cousin Louis to tell him about Dad; I told him to not let my mother leave his mother's house and I would be there shortly to tell her. It was the longest ride ever from Scranton to Pittston. I thought, *How am I going to do this? How do I tell this woman, who was with this man for fifty-nine years, that she's alone now?* It was the hardest thing I've ever had to tell someone. I arrived at my aunt's. My cousin Louis lives next door, and he walked across the front yard when he saw my car pull up. We embraced and I composed myself for Mom's sake. When I walked in, the twins were fussing in the kitchen, doing supper dishes. Mom turned around when I walked through the front door, and asked "What are you doing here? Why aren't you at work?" I just looked at her, eyes swelling up with tears, and she knew. I went home that night knowing one third of our threesome family was gone, hoping Mom would be okay in the weeks to follow and that she would adjust. I walked up the steps from my garage into my kitchen. My son was seven years old at the time. He was lying on the couch with his dad. I said, "Hello guys, how's my big boy doing?" He looked at me and said, "I heard all about grandpa. I know you're very sad about your father, and

I'm very sorry Mommy. Grandpa is in a better place now." And there you have it, the perspective from the eyes of a seven-year-old.

I felt a great deal of guilt in the months that followed my father's death, asking myself if I did the right thing for his healthcare needs; I was the power of attorney and in charge of making medical decisions. I had been in the healthcare field many, many years and knew he was shutting down. There was no recovery. I knew this but often wondered if my mother understood what I was trying to tell her every day he was in the hospital. I told her we were just going to take this one day at a time. I reinforced that if he didn't come back home, if he didn't recover, that she would be okay and would always have me, her sisters, and all her nieces and nephews that loved her unconditionally. She would never be alone.

Hospice has a "service," where at least once a month a nurse calls to see how the family is coping. I had numerous conversations with the nurses there, about my guilt. Did I do the right thing by putting him in hospice? My brain tells me yes, because I knew the end of his life was near, but my heart always disagreed. I held so much guilt that I left there to go to work in the afternoon. *Really? Why the hell didn't I just stay?*

Was my hospital going to close its doors if I called off? No one from our family was there when he passed away. He was only in hospice from Thursday to Sunday. As time went on I forgave myself. I did the best I could for Dad and I know he knew it. My focus for the next eighteen months was on my mom. I continued to be the best daughter I could, because I just wanted her to be okay.

Last week was the Bloomsburg Fair. Anyone who lives in Northeastern Pennsylvania or surrounding areas knows about the fair. It's held the last week of September in a college town about an hour and fifteen minutes from where I grew up. The fair is held on a very large piece of land and attracts a tremendous amount of visitors from all over. It features all kinds of food, amusements, livestock, and a whole host of displays from local vendors and artists. When I was growing up, it was a yearly tradition to skip school and go to the fair. I guess we thought it would be less crowded than on a weekend. So off we went. My uncle

Jimmy Fitzpatrick drove a wood-paneled station wagon, and my mom and I tagged along with my uncle, my aunt MaryLou, and cousins Jimmy, Tammy, and Amy. Amy was very young at the time and probably only went once or twice before we stopped going. We loaded in that station wagon and looked forward to the adventure. My favorite attraction was the livestock. As smelly as it was, I loved the prize cows, sheep, goats, chickens and alpacas. My son is like me; he loves to see animals too, no matter what they are. They always had these long buildings we would refer to as "barracks," and inside were vendors and displays of all sorts. Some of these buildings were sponsored by church groups and served homemade dinners, family style. That's where we always ate. For a very reasonable price, we ate a delicious home-cooked meal, usually the turkey dinner. Afterwards we strolled all over the fairgrounds, munching on junk! But it wasn't junk to us at the time...it was dessert! If my cousin Jimmy and I had any money of our own, we scoured the place for a souvenir. One year I bought a turquoise and silver ring. I had that ring for years. That was perhaps the beginning of my love for jewelry -- and I haven't stopped yet! We didn't go on many rides. I really don't care for any ride that goes too fast or whips around or hangs you upside down. Nope, not for Tina. But the "Sky Ride" was for me. We just hopped inside the carriage and up we went, holding onto the bar that locked in place in front of us. With our feet dangling (I always feared I would lose a shoe and have to walk around with one shoe), we observed the thousands of people below us and the fairgrounds. It dropped us off at the other end of the park and we walked back what seemed like miles when we were so young.

My mother and her sister MaryLou were attracted to the vendors who were selling gadgets of every kind imaginable. One year, they fell for it. They invested in the VitaMix, a super duper, spectacular, stupendous, can't-live-without...blender. And it wasn't cheap! I'm talking $75 dollars back in 1975! We stood and watched this guy give a demonstration to the crowd of women for a half hour. It could do everything except mow the lawn! He made us taste the fruits of his labor in tiny paper cups - I believe it was some sort of sorbet. This blender could make puree for soups, ice cream, sorbet, all kinds of juices...they just HAD to have it. So Mom lugged it around the rest of the day, and she warned me, "And don't tell your father how much it was." What the heck did I care? All I cared about was the fact that she was going to make these delicious things with this machine, including homemade sherbet. I'm here to tell you that that ugly looking blender never made me sherbet or anything else as far as that goes. She used it as a regular blender, no different than any blender she could have bought at Jewelcor or Strouds at that time for about thirty dollars. So, down the cellar it went to collect dust. Twenty years later, she gave it to my cousin Jimmy who thought he could use it. He took it home and the motor sounded like it had marbles stuck in it; it was dead. The must-have VitaMix was put to rest in the garbage. Good times, good times.

We left the Bloomsburg Fair looking forward to next year and a day skipped from school. We piled into the station wagon, Uncle Jimmy behind the wheel, driving Route 11 in the dark all the way back to Pittston and West Pittston. Us three kids (And later four, with Amy) laid in the back of the station wagon (no need for seat belts or anything, we were good). We changed into our pajamas in the car because, "It's going to be late by the time we get home." I guess walking around an entire day at a fair, touching everything in sight and riding rides, didn't warrant a bath before bed, but who were we to argue? We were just kids. Kids living a good life with parents who loved us and enjoyed taking us to places like the Bloomsburg Fair.

Five years ago, on a Friday afternoon, I picked Philip up from school at three o'clock. We hadn't any plans, so when he got in my car I told him we were going to the Bloomsburg Fair. "Now?" he said. "Yes, now." He had never been there, and I hadn't been there since I was a young teenager. He was in sixth grade. I showed him everything I used to love to see when I was younger. Oddly enough, the first thing he wanted to see was the livestock! He spent a good amount of time in the barns. It brought back so many lovely memories for me of what a great childhood I had. We had something to eat, we had some junk, and we went into those barracks to walk around all the crafts and displays. I didn't see any church-run family dinners, but we still managed to indulge in fair food anyway. Before we left, we did one last thing. We took the sky ride from one end of the fairgrounds to the other and walked back. It seemed even longer because I'm old! We took our time walking back and had to remember where we had parked. We made it back home by ten o'clock that night; it was just enough time for me to show him a part of my childhood. I, however, did not make him put his pajamas on in the car; he sat up front with me, wore his seatbelt, and showered when we got home. Times have changed. Last weekend, Philip went to the fair with two friends of his from school. For new drivers, they were driving a good distance to get there. I was nervous all day waiting to hear from him. I lectured him for days before about staying together, not talking to strangers, knowing where his money is, and watching for deer on the drive home because it would be dark and maybe a bit foggy. He made it home by seven thirty and texted me to tell me the three of them were in Pittston but at Perkins "for some proper food." I had to laugh to myself. I guess I did something right; we don't eat a lot of junk food and he knows the difference. He had a wonderful day with his friends and that made me happy.

❦ ❦ ❦

I know there's an old saying, "You can't teach an old dog new tricks," but I've come to realize that even as we get older, we learn new things. We're constantly learning in our day-to-day endeavors. It amazes me how much our brains can hold. We learn new goals and new techniques at our jobs. We learn to raise a child in an ever-changing world and hope we teach them right from wrong and set a good example for them. We learn how to take the steps needed for ourselves, to live a life of sound mind and healthy being. Life is basically a learning curve, and our views adapt from day to day. When we are young and still under the influence of our parents, we learn from them. After you are married, you learn from each other as you grow and mature. And in my case I learned to change again after my divorce. I learned to speak my mind; I learned to rely on only myself; I learned those that truly love you are the ones that will stick around when the dust settles and will put up with all of your ups and downs, bad moods, bouts of sadness, and loneliness. I can thank my cousins and my intimate circle of friends for being there for me when I needed them the most. I've also learned that others will judge me no matter what I do. You would think that would not matter to me anymore, but at times it still does. I still fall prey to the concept of "always doing the right thing" for everyone, when in reality I should only worry about doing what's right for me. I was never one to hide emotions or feelings. I guess you can say I was always one of those people who wears her heart on her sleeve, perhaps without saying any words, but it showed in my facial expressions and in my eyes. I have learned, at this ripe age of fifty-four, to channel my inner emotions to verbal expressions. Some may find this offensive and perhaps a tiny bit disrespectful; however, I do it without malice and with enough tact that it shouldn't be an issue. I firmly believe there are ways to say something and still get a point across if done with kindness. Usually, these people who react negatively never hold back what they think themselves, but because they don't recognize this new person inside of me, all of a sudden I'm expressing out of turn. What I also find interesting is that when challenged, they often back down and try to explain themselves. Words are a marvelous entity but they can also hurt. Tone and inflection are crucial to how we interpret what's being said. "Tact is the ability to tell someone to go to hell, and they look forward to the trip." My cousin Amy first showed me that quote and I love it.

I don't stick my nose in anyone's business, and I mind my own, generally speaking, unless it has a direct affect on me. The only nose-sticking I do is in my son's life, because he is still young and my responsibility. Other than that…"to each his own," like Carmelita used to say. She had another saying that would fit this scenario, but I'll keep that one to myself!

My life has suddenly become busy, stressful at times, tiring and frustrating, too. I have trouble falling asleep some nights worrying about crap that I cannot fix, because it already happened or hasn't happened yet. Then I look over at my clock and count how many hours until my alarm goes off and get even more anxious. I know in my mind I no longer have to answer to anyone and what I do or say is my business. However, my heart sometimes steps in and makes me question myself. I have a bad habit of perseverating on incidents, taking them to heart and desperately trying to resolve them. Well, I have realized lately that all things cannot be resolved by Tina. If someone has a problem with what I say, do, or how I react, these are your issues, not mine. There is an abundance of stress and disappointment and problems in this country today and in all of our lives, and quite frankly, I can do without any added drama. I still believe in the traditional system of ethics: be kind, be loving, be sympathetic, be gentle, be forgiving, keep an open mind, and until you've walked a mile in my moccasins, don't judge. In the end, we all will leave

this earth -- we may have to answer to a higher being if you are religious

-- and we all want to be remembered in a good light. I am still a work in

progress. I am an old dog still learning new tricks.

❦ ❦ ❦

Love. What is love? The age-old question that many people,

theologians, and saints have tried to explain or answer. We all have our

own experiences with love and all think we know what love is. We can

love our dog, love our profession, love our home, love our family, love

our children, love our spouses or significant others, and maybe even love

ourselves. For each and every person on this earth love has its own

definition and its own role to play in our lives. I have always loved the

reading "The First Letter of Saint Paul to the Corinthians," which I have

heard many times in church and especially at weddings; in fact, it was

read at my own wedding in 1988. It really is one of my favorites: "Love

is patient, love is kind, it is not jealous, it is not pompous, it is not

inflated, it is not rude. It bears all things, believes all things, hopes all things, endures all things. Love never fails." That is the extremely shortened version; it's quite beautiful and insightful in its entirety. If only every one of us tried to live by St. Paul's words, what a lovely world we would be living in. However, somewhere in that beautiful prayer, we need the word "trust." Trust is just as significant as love. I'm not sure if St. Paul ever did, but I wish he wrote letters about trust. Either way, his words are very true and if you read the whole letter, you will have a better understanding of love through his eyes.

My therapist told me recently that the Eskimos have twenty-five different words for snow. I'm not certain if it's actually twenty-five different words or twenty-five different words to describe snow. After all, snow is their life. This woman posed the question to me, "wouldn't it be great if we had twenty-five different words for love?" I thought about that, and although there may not be that many words for love, all of us in some form or fashion have experienced different kinds of love or different degrees of love. The Greeks have several different words for love. My favorite four are these: EROS, romantic, passionate love that leads you to tell someone "I love you." PHILIA, relating to a close friendship. STORGE, unconditional love for family. AGAPE, to show empathy and a universal love, including love of thy self. All four of these words are significant, and perhaps we all need to practice them in our everyday life.

This topic of conversation came up in one of my therapy sessions. I was trying to figure out why I still grieve over my divorce at times. Obviously, it was the right thing to do considering the circumstances, and I no longer love my ex-husband as a wife would love a husband, and he no longer loves me as a husband would love a wife. Five years have passed since we've lived in the same house, trust is non-existent, and the waters are too muddy. Then why? That's when she told me about the Eskimos. I did not love the relationship we had the last few years before the divorce, and I did not love the changes that were taking place before my eyes. We, my therapist and I, decided I was in love with the whole idea that my plan of how I saw my life to be, the plan of how my future was supposed to be, and the promise that was made on that altar. It had been taken away from me and I still harbor resentment and a bit of anger for that. So without loving the man, as it would be if we had remained married, I still become melancholy over what my vision of our life was supposed to be, as a family. I miss having my family, the three of us. I still feel I do not have closure. You would think that signing those divorce papers is closure, but it's not, at least not for me. Of course he knows how I feel because we signed those papers, but we took two years to do that, because I hoped counseling would fix it all. I could not forgive. I cannot forgive. He had no trust, and then circumstances led me to have no trust, and that's a biggie. The hurt is deeper than that. It's a wound that opens without forewarning and has to begin the healing process over and over again. In my life, I am surrounded by love, and I'm eternally grateful to those individuals in my life who offer unconditional love to me every day.

During our separation, I had people tell me, "Wait until the word gets out that you are single; you will not be alone for long. Men will show interest because you have so much to offer, and they are going to want to get to know you." That never meant much to me. I just wanted to be alone. I didn't care about men wanting to talk to me; it just wasn't important to me. I had so much to deal with at hand that I did not need anymore issues. I spent a lot of time alone in the beginning. I needed that time to wrap my thoughts around what was going on and how to make a plan to move forward. As time went by, there were a few men who reached out to me via texting and phone calls. Not strangers, but guys I knew for a very long time. I soon realized that these men did not genuinely care about me; they were just curious. I think that if I died tomorrow they would probably attend my funeral out of respect, and they may care about my well being, but really that's where it ends. And that's ok. I needed the flirting and the attention to give me some confidence back. I needed to feel wanted and desirable, because that was missing for quite some time in my marriage. And honestly, it felt good. These were not real relationships, but just an affirmation that as a woman, I can still be attractive to the opposite sex. It made me feel good inside, for as fleeting as that time was, and gave me the self-esteem I needed to face this new life. St. Paul wrote to the Corinthians, "If I have the gift of prophecy and all knowledge; if I have all faith as to move mountains, but do not have love, I am nothing." Love those close to you; tell them as often as you could. Show them you love them with your daily deeds so they feel secure and loved and they will love you ten-fold in return. Don't be shy to say those three important words. Appreciate those in your life that make your life complete. Trust one another...it's never a sign of weakness, but one of being secure with yourself. And remember, without love, we are nothing.

It is now November, two weeks away from Thanksgiving. Growing up, Thanksgiving was a pretty big deal in my family. Our valley had a big rivalry football game between Wyoming Area (my alma mater) and Pittston Area. The two high schools have been rivals for years -- way back to my parents' time! Thanksgiving dinner was always planned *after* the big game. It was usually at my Aunt Sara's and Uncle Skippy's house with eighteen or so of us at two big long tables set up in her finished basement. Two weeks ago the WA vs PA game was held at Pittston Area stadium. Over the years it has been changed to a different date; it's now in the evening instead of Thanksgiving afternoon and three weeks or so before Thanksgiving. This kind of takes away the whole excitement I feel, or maybe it's just because it was tradition. It didn't matter how cold it was or that everyone was hungry for that turkey dinner. The only problem was that I was the only cousin in my family that lived in West Pittston and attended Wyoming Area schools, and the Pittston Area football team, aka the Patriots, beat the Wyoming Area Warriors every single year. I'd go to the game in my younger years with my Dad and, embarrassing as it was, he made me sit with him on the Pittston Area side. He was born and raised in Pittston and it was his alma mater. Boy oh boy, there I sat with him, watching my friends across the football field; I felt like a traitor! They beat us every single year. Then the game was over and I had to face all my cousins at dinner. Picture this: My oldest cousin Tommy was a football player for the Patriots. His sister, my cousin Mary Ellen, was a cheerleader for the Patriots, and although we were having dinner with my mom's side of the family, my cousin Tina Marie was in the marching band for…Yes, you guessed it, the Patriots. I was outnumbered by the victorious Patriots. Let the teasing begin! I can laugh about it now, and I know they were kidding with me, but as soon as we would walk in my Aunt Sara's door, it would begin."What happened to your Warriors?" Hahaha. Well, as my senior year approached, our team had an undefeated season. I thought to myself this may just be the year for WA. And low and behold...we beat the Patriots! We even made it to the championship, following that Thanksgiving game.

About two weeks ago, they held the annual rivalry game. I didn't go, but kind of wished I had. I will make a point to go next year. I have a dilemma now, though. I have lived on the east side of the great Susquehanna River (the Pittston side) for twenty-five years now, and my son attended Pittston Area schools up to the seventh grade. Hmmm, which school do I root for? I'm sure my classmates would tell me, "Once a Warrior, always a Warrior." I'm torn. The next morning, following the game, my boyfriend John informed me that Wyoming Area defeated Pittston Area in a huge upset. Shouldn't have been a surprise; they led an undefeated season to that night. When I heard what the score was, I decided that once again, I was a Warrior.

🐿 🐿 🐿

Today is November 19, 2018. Thanksgiving is a time for giving thanks and sharing the day with your loved ones, whether it be family or friends. I am working Thanksgiving this year. Working in the healthcare world, I miss out on weekends, holidays, special events, and quality time with family. Sometimes holidays are the only time when the whole family gets the opportunity to spend the day or evening together. I miss out on plenty of those endearing moments, more than I care to count. I don't remember if I even realized that I'd be sacrificing these times when I chose this profession. Perhaps I was too young to know this. When I finished my medical technology internship in 1988, I was immediately hired by the American Red Cross Blood Services in the Infectious Disease laboratory. I accepted this position, as did two other girls in my class, because it did not involve weekends or holidays. The money was a few dollars less than our other thirteen classmates who took jobs in various hospitals from here to Philadelphia, but to me, it was well worth it in order to have a normal life with my soon-to-be husband. Here I am thirty-one years later and I have been giving up every other weekend and three holidays a year for the past fifteen years in order to earn a decent living. The medical profession only recognizes six holidays a year: Thanksgiving, Christmas Day, New Year's Day, Memorial Day, Fourth of July, and Labor Day. There is no such thing as Easter Sunday, Mother's Day, Father's Day, President's Day, Martin Luther King Day, or Columbus Day. And if you celebrate any other holidays, for example Rosh Hashanah, Yom Kippur, or Kwanza, you're out of luck. If you want those days to celebrate, you must use a vacation day. I don't think the majority of society realizes what the health professionals give up in order to keep a hospital or nursing home or rehabilitation center going. Before I got my "real job," I worked in a skilled nursing home facility, and I worked weekends and plenty of holidays then also. I have been giving up that special family time since 1982. I am so tired of it. When I was on the second shift, I went to Christmas dinner in my scrubs and gobbled down my meal without really even tasting how delicious it probably was, because I had to be the first one to get up from the table and leave for work. Now that I work day shift, I leave the house before my son is even awake. Last Christmas day he was alone at our house on Christmas morning until he went to see his grandparents next door in the afternoon. I realize it's not the end of the world, and I should be grateful that I am employed and my son is the most understanding young man I have ever known, but it's hard. I find it very emotional to be working while my family is home enjoying each other and I am not there. So many people express their dismay at department stores being open on Thanksgiving and New Year's Day, and try to discourage shoppers from patronizing on the holiday. No one expresses their appreciation for the healthcare society for taking care of loved ones in the hospital, traumas from those involved in accidents traveling during the holidays, or those that come into the emergency room sick. We give of ourselves. We give up our special family time that is shared during a holiday. We miss out on our children and the enjoyment they have on Christmas morning or Fourth of July with cookouts and firework displays. We give up a hell of a lot. I chose this profession. I will probably be doing this work until I can retire in eleven years. There are going to be many many more weekends and holidays I miss and family occasions I was unable to share. My coworkers and I had a similar discussion last week, how we plan our lives around our weekend and holiday schedule. Every time I get invited to a party, a dinner, a wedding, a graduation party, my first response is always the same, "Let me see if that's my weekend to work." We work every other weekend at my hospital, which leaves only two weekends a month to live our lives and attend a social gathering. Do you know what is the most pathetic of all? When a loved one passes away and you sit quietly hoping the family has the funeral on your day off or your weekend off. Very sad. No one really understands that to request a weekend off is a big deal. And forget about holidays, you cannot request to have it off; you must switch with a coworker which hardly ever works out. My life is ruled by my weekends to work. So this Thanksgiving, please give thanks that you have dedicated, dependable healthcare workers out there waiting to take care of you or your loved ones if need be, to ambulance drivers, paramedics, police officers, nurses and doctors and to all the professionals who give up their family life on weekends and holidays.

❦ ❦ ❦

I have the greatest in-laws ever. It's been almost three years since my divorce was final and almost five years since my ex-husband and I separated, and my in-laws and I still have a wonderful relationship. I live next door to them, and if you know where I live, we are really close neighbors. We can have a normal conversation from porch to porch. I remained in our home, which was built by Mom's father, since the separation. I own this home now. I'm not sure if this was my choice to stay, but it happened that way when my ex-husband moved out while we were in counseling; perhaps he was thinking that things would work out and he'd be back here, but that did not happen. I had friends tell me that I needed to move so as not to be so close to my in-laws, but I felt it was the right thing to do for my son; I wanted him to be close to his grandparents and it would keep some sort of normalcy to his young life. He was eleven at the time. My parents were already gone, and Mom and Dad were his only set of grandparents left. The day I got engaged in 1987 was the day I asked my in-laws if it would be okay for me to begin calling them Mom and Dad. "Of course!" they said. I never understood people that couldn't bring themselves to call their in-laws Mom and Dad. I suppose it's perfectly acceptable to call them by their first names, but there are people out there who continue to refer to their in-laws as Mr. or Mrs. so-and-so. To each his own as Carmelita would say. I knew I wanted to call them Mom and Dad. We had a close relationship for thirty-one years and remarkably still do. They know how much I love them and I believe they still love me as a daughter.

One afternoon, after we separated, I got a phone call from Mom. She was emotional and spoke to me from her heart. She plainly told me that she so hoped that we could work things out for Philip's sake and for our family, asking me to please try and reconnect and settle our differences. However, she said, "You are beautiful and kind and have so much love to give. You deserve to be happy and if it doesn't work out, I hope you find someone someday that will love you the way you deserve to be loved." She also said, "As women we forgive, but we don't forget." She wanted me to know that she and Dad will always be here for me and their grandson, for whatever we may need, and they will never turn their backs on us. I cried; she cried. I have never forgotten that phone call, obviously, and to this day, five years later, she and Dad have held their promise to my son and I, tenfold. I often tell her, "You are stuck with me forever Mom," and her response is always the same… "And I'm thankful for that." I love my in-laws dearly and I made a promise to them and to their son that I am always here for them too, and I will take care of them as best I can. I will do anything for them that they need me to do. I am not doing these things to relieve my ex-husband or my ex-sister-in-law of their duties for their parents, but I do it out of my heart and my love for Mom and Dad. My parents are gone; now MaryFrances and Phil are my parents.

Most people do not understand this relationship. Some have even said, "You are not obligated to them anymore; you're divorced." They tell me, "Cut the apron strings;" not for any other reason except that I am no longer with their son and this should be where it stops. I cannot and will not do that. I have been in this family since 1987. I do it for my son too. I want him to see that even with adversity and changes in life, certain things can remain the same. I know he sees and realizes what I do for my parents and he thanks me for it occasionally. One day, I was talking about retirement, and I happen to say that when I retire in ten or eleven years, I am planning on moving to a warmer climate, probably Florida. He turned to me and said, "But what about Grandma and Grandpa?" I looked at him and said, "Honey, I love Grandma and Grandpa with all of my heart, but they are not my responsibility entirely. They have your father and your aunt Lisa." Plus I don't think that at that moment he stopped to think that they will be in their late 80s and early 90s by then. It really touched my heart to hear him pose that question though, because at that second in time, I knew he realized how much I love his grandparents and how I have not abandoned them nor them us. I am very blessed to have two individuals who are not blood-related care so much for me, a daughter-in-law, an "ex" daughter-in-law, if we are getting specific. There was a time when I was at the lunch table with co-workers who were complaining about in-laws. I remained quiet; I had nothing to contribute to the conversation. Then one of my friends said, "Oh, don't even ask Tina about her in-laws. She's the only one here that has a great relationship with in-laws." They were correct, I have a wonderful bond with Mom and Dad.

I am certainly aware that it didn't have to be this way. They could have cut their ties with me, and I would have understood that, for their son's sake. But they are outstanding individuals and included me in several dinners and gatherings even after the divorce. I went because I love them, and I appreciate the fact that they thought of me and for the sake of my son to set the example that we are trying the best we could to maintain some sort of normalcy of a family considering the circumstances. But, as expected, time is going on, and I'm not included anymore, except for my nephews' graduations, and I'm okay with that. I understand. It is probably getting too uncomfortable now since I have a significant other in my life. They have met John and have spoken to him, and when I went away with my son last summer and John stayed at my house to care for my dog Elsa, they offered John to use their grill if he wanted to make himself a hamburger. They are pretty outstanding people. They have never once stopped me from walking into their home to check in on them, and therefore I try to go next door a few times a week. When

I don't, I make sure I call and talk to them. I do not go to the grocery store without first calling to see if they need anything, and Mom feels comfortable enough to call and ask me to pick up prescriptions from the drugstore on my way home from work. They do so much for us and I will never be able to thank them enough for their generosity, their love, and the stability they have given my son. It takes a tremendous amount of courage and strength to do that and still not make it appear that they are going against their son. It's never been about taking sides here. It's only always been about love and respect for one another. They even understand that I do have someone in my life and I am receiving the love and honor that I deserve. We have a mutual understanding of how our relationship works and how to maintain it. I am grateful, I am blessed, and I am extremely fortunate to have these two wonderful people in my life. I love you Mary Frances. I love you Phil. Mom and Dad, thank you for all you do for me and your grandson.

My father had one sister, Rose, or Aunt Rosie. Aunt Rosie was younger than my father by just a few years, and she was the apple of his eye. He loved his sister, and they had a mutually respectful relationship. My mother had a very loving relationship with Rosie. Mom had three sisters of her own, and Aunt Rosie was a fourth sister to her. They called each other almost every day and on Sundays, especially after Uncle Joe passed away, my aunt had Sunday dinner with us. Mom and Aunt Rosie spent time together and I knew they loved each other. It's not often sisters-in-law have such a close relationship. I often hoped I would have a close relationship with my ex-sister-in-law, but it just wasn't quite like that. Aunt Rosie was strict in her mannerisms, much like her brother, but she had a heart of gold and gave unconditionally to her family; her daughter, my cousin Tina Marie is exactly like her in that way. Aunt Rosie and Uncle Joe had two children, Charlie and Tina Marie. They lived in Trenton, New Jersey for many years in a ranch house with a "breezeway"...I just had to say that because as a child I had never heard of a breezeway, nor did I know what it was until I saw their house. A breezeway is a concrete pathway leading from the core of the house straight to the garage. In that garage, I remember a huge poster of my

Uncle Joe holding a bowling ball; he was in a bowling league and the picture was taken and blown up to depict him bowling a 300! I can remember riding bikes around the block on Hamilton Square and being scared to death of the neighbor's German Shepherd behind the chain link fence, pacing and barking as we rode by. Who would've thought I'd end up raising German Shepherds!

Growing up in West Pittston, where most homes were two- and three-story century homes, a ranch home was rare. My mom and dad always told me that the first big road trip they took me on when they got me was to Trenton to see Aunt Rosie and Uncle Joe and my new cousins. I have many pictures in my baby album that my mom made of me at my cousins' house. One of my favorites is of Tina Marie and me as infants in an inflatable swimming pool with my mom holding me as I was sitting in the pool and Uncle Joe holding Tina -- all of us, smiling! Very happy little girls and very loving parents. There is another of Tina Marie and me in their front yard with our cute little sundresses on, wearing white sneakers, and my Uncle Joe's company van in the background reading Bromley Heating Company.

My Aunt Rosie was a very proper, sophisticated, hard-working woman. She was a spotless housekeeper and as my mom would often say, "Rosie is as neat as a pin." I think that must be an old saying, because I don't hear it much anymore, but that's how she let me know that Aunt Rosie was a put-together woman. She was not a gossiper and had nothing bad to say about anyone, and even if there was something bothering her, I don't believe she was one to confront people. She was strict in her values and always did the right thing. Perhaps I didn't appreciate this until my older mature days when I knew I could confide anything in her and she would give me motherly advice. My father and I often butted heads in his older years; he was a stubborn man. I would call her to vent and she always had a sympathetic ear for me. She knew him well…she was his sister.

Aunt Rosie was impeccable with her appearance -- the way she dressed, her hair, and the way she presented herself. She was soft-spoken and I probably only heard her raise her voice a time or two in my whole life. One summer I went to stay in Trenton for a week for a little vacation. I was probably about eight years old or so. My cousin Tina is a year older so we always played well together and I loved spending time with her. I think I must have been going through a stubborn stage because during that particular trip; I really showed my true colors. I had always been a very picky eater and there was a stage in my young life where all I ate were peanut butter and jelly sandwiches for all my meals. And by the way, it's still my favorite sandwich, just not for every meal! One evening, my aunt prepared a very nice supper for us and I wanted no part of it. I sat there and wouldn't eat a blessed thing. I wanted a peanut butter and jelly sandwich. Well, the battle of wills ensued. I was the last one at the table and I was told if I didn't eat something, I couldn't go across the street to play dolls with Tina Marie and her friends. Gosh, I don't recall at what point she gave in, but I was excused from the table eventually. Through the years, if we were reminiscing about Trenton, I often brought this story up. We would chuckle and make light of it. However, a few years before my aunt passed away, we were all together and I once more told that story. The next day, she called and asked me if I thought she was mean and if I was holding that against her all these years later. Oh my gosh, never! I felt like an ass for having told that story. I used to tell it because I couldn't believe what a stubborn little brat I had been to her. She didn't deserve that. She was always so good to me. And that's exactly what I told her. I never ever meant to hurt her feelings. I could never hurt her; I loved her. She was the most genuine human being to walk this earth. I apologized. I think she was okay with me saying I was sorry, but you can be sure I never told that story ever again until just now. Sometimes we say things, thinking we are doing it for one reason, and the intention is often misunderstood and taken to heart. This was the case in this situation. On a lighter note, we have home movies of Aunt Rosie with curlers in her hair, trying to avoid being filmed and thinking she could hide behind a recliner and not be seen! Now that is something we all laughed at! A very proud woman, especially how she looked, being seen in big rollers certainly was a sight! And to have it on film...priceless.

My parents and I made many trips to Trenton, and my mom always bragged that my aunt Rosie made the best roast she ever tasted! She was indeed a great cook, and my Uncle Joe loved to cook too; his specialty happened to be Italian potato salad. His job was to cut the roast beef. Aunt Rosie, Uncle Joe, and my cousins Charlie and Tina Marie moved to Pittston in the 1970s after the 1972 Agnes Flood. They bought a home in Jenkins Township and lived there until my uncle passed away in 1985. My aunt then sold her home and moved into an apartment which was very close to her daughter and her family. My cousin Charlie went to college in Boston, became an architect, and has a successful firm in Pennsylvania, outside of Philadelphia. She was very proud of her children's success, and by all means she should've been.

My dear aunt passed away in 2008 after a courageous battle with lung cancer, her daughter Tina Marie taking care of her every step along the way. She certainly didn't deserve this; she was too good of a person. My mom, my son Philip and I went to visit her one day in November, right before Thanksgiving. She was so happy to see Philip; he was only six years old at the time. It was a nice visit, but she looked so frail. She had lost so much weight. I have pictures of that day and it pains me to look at her that way. It's not the way she looked all her life, so I try to remember how she looked all the years I knew her growing up. One day I had her in the car with me; I was taking her to a doctor's appointment where Tina Marie would be meeting us. She looked at me and said, "I'm going to beat this cancer, Tina Louise." I wish she had. The same evening, after I visited her with my mom and Philip, Aunt Rosie passed away. I think of her often and she will be in my heart always.

Today is Monday, November 18, 2019. Eleven years ago today, my warm-hearted Aunt Rosie Maira passed away. I was reminded of this day, this morning while talking to her daughter, my cousin Tina Marie. Isn't it something, how we feel when the anniversary of a loved one's passing comes upon us every year and it takes us right back to that day? It just happens that way. Tina Marie was very melancholy this morning, and I know how she feels. We are both parent-less. We miss them all the time. There's that unavoidable void present, and what is left is our fond memories. We honor them by thinking of them and what they gave to us, talking about them with a loved one, or visiting them at the cemetery. Either way, they come to our mind and tug at our heart because we loved them dearly and they are no longer here with us. Aunt Rosie was a very special woman in my eyes. She was my confidante as I matured, and with her soft voice I knew she loved me. I loved her dearly, too.

Christmas and New Year's Day have recently passed, another year gone by, another year of changes, another year of memories made. Although I worked both Christmas Eve and New Year's Day, I made it a point to plan my annual Christmas party here at my home with my family; we were thirty in all. I worry every year because my home is small and maybe not everyone will have a seat at the table in my kitchen, but I set up card tables in the other rooms and a banquet table alongside my kitchen table. My home is lived in, so I'm perfectly fine with people taking their plates and eating in my living rooms. I just want everyone to feel comfortable and at home here. I know in my heart that no one cares about the size of my home, because all that matters is that we are together under one roof that one time a year, other than a funeral or a wedding. I enjoy having them here and I know they appreciate my effort. Most importantly, I am making great memories for Philip. He asks me every year if we will be having the family Christmas party so I know he loves it too. My cousin MaryEllen and her family were all here from Ecuador and Holland throughout the holidays, and we celebrated the union of two hearts at my cousin Amy and Mike's wedding, a beautiful new beginning for the two of them. My son and I joined John's family for a lovely

Christmas lunch at his parents home, and then the three of us enjoyed a most delicious Christmas evening dinner at my cousin Tina Marie and Joe's home. She made homemade manicotti that my Grandmother Tuttilmond taught her how to make and they were out of this world! Her brother, my cousin Charlie, and his daughter were with us and it made the day even more special. I watched as Charlie jumped right in and helped my cousin Tina Marie with the dinner. He sliced up two long loaves of French bread to make his own garlic bread to have with the manicotti and he did it with such finesse that you'd have thought he was a professional chef. It was cut and seasoned to perfection. I guess that's why he's such a successful architect; his passion for his work makes him a perfectionist. He reminded me of his Dad, my uncle Joe, who also liked to be in the kitchen helping to cook. It was heartwarming to see this.

I attended Christmas Eve mass at ten o'clock and felt the sentimental feelings that I always tend to have at that mass. The choir sounded wonderful, and the music always moves me to have a lump in my throat. I hold back the tears. I can't explain why I feel this way; I think perhaps the melody and the words are so touching and allow us all to briefly forget the troubles in our lives and in our world and just appreciate the fact that we are there remembering the story of the birth of our Lord.

I spent New Year's Eve with my high school classmates at my longtime friend Donna's home. Never in my dreams would I have imagined that I would have been with individuals I knew thirty-eight years ago, but really did not have relationships with until five years ago. I am truly blessed with my circle of friends. As a child, New Year's Eve was very exciting. We usually spent it all together and had delicious food and drinks. We sat around in the living room, on couches and recliners and with kids all over the floor. We watched the crystal ball drop with a countdown from New York City and listened to Guy Lombardo and his orchestra play beautiful music on TV. Then the ball dropped and came to a halt…it was New Year's Day! Exactly midnight! Each of us would grab an old pot and lid or a wooden spoon, and our parents would send us outside to "bang the pots." I could laugh out loud just typing this. I'm not quite sure what that signified other than a hell of a lot of noise in the neighborhood, but that was our version of fireworks I guess. One such year we celebrated at my Aunt Sara and Uncle Skippy's house on Nafus

Street in Pittston. There we were, anxiously waiting for midnight, and then when it finally happened, we took our pots and went outside. Only one little mistake though -- someone grabbed a new pot of Aunt Sara's and banged the hell out of it with the lid! It was so dented that she had to throw it away. We will never forget that story and that particular night -- she reminded us every year, and we laughed about it every year. But that's how memories are made. I'm fifty-five and still remember, another reason to continue to tell stories and even write the stories so our present day generations can hear them and hopefully remember them and tell them to their children.

During the holidays, we had losses too. One of my best friends Susan lost her dad a few days before Christmas, and my godfather Angelo lost his wife Ellen right after New Year's after a three-year battle with Alzheimer's. My heart goes out to Susan; her birthday is on Christmas Day and she lost her twin sister a few years back. This is what makes holidays hard, not just for her but for a lot of us. I tend to have an open heart and listening ear for people in my life that may feel anxious, stressed, and even depressed during the holidays, because it is real.

Sometimes it's just too much. I had this conversation with my cousin Tammy during the holiday and she hit the nail on the head. As women, how could we not be stressed? Almost all of the time, it's us who cleans the house in preparation for Christmas, we do all the gift buying, send out the cards, wrap the gifts, decorate the house, food shop for the big day, cook the special meal, and then clean up -- all while still working and worrying about how much money we are spending. It's a huge deal. Somehow, we manage it, and when it's all coming to an end all we can say is "I can't wait for Christmas to be over." It's a shame to even say it, but I know just about all women say it, maybe not out loud, but I just said it for you. I wish there was an easier way to not feel the pressures. If I find one, I'll let you all know. But for now, we do what we do to make the holidays as special as we possibly can, because it's all for the love we have for our families, and we wouldn't want it any other way.

❦ ❦ ❦

We often drove to New Jersey to visit relatives in Leonia, Trenton and Lake Hiawatha when I was a child. This was before Interstate 80.

The popular road was Route 46. It still exists today, but I think people use it as an alternative route because I-80 is so much faster. Along Route 46, there was a popular stop called Hot Dog Johnny's. It wasn't more than a pop-up stand with a pavilion and picnic tables, but if you were traveling that route, you stopped for a hot dog and a cold glass mug of birch beer. I was young, but I remember stopping there with my parents. Two weeks ago, John and I took a road trip to Long Island and we turned off I-80 and headed to Hot Dog Johnny's. It's still there and busy as ever. The walls are enclosed for the winter weather and it was standing room only as we waited in line to give our order. I'm not going to say it's the best dog I've ever had, because I'm not really a hot dog aficionado (my mother and her sisters were, though. They loved going for "dirty ol' hot dogs with everything on them"), but it was tasty and the birch beer and french fries were really good. We took pictures, and now I have the memory.

It's winter and although the weathermen predicted an early morning snowfall, it started late this afternoon. It's still falling and accumulating as I type. I always loved the snow growing up, and not because I skied or ice skated, but I just thought everything looked so clean and beautiful and picturesque in our yard. I loved to shovel snow and felt so good taking deep breaths of crisp air. I still love those aspects of winter, but now, winter is a lot of work for me. I'm always conscious to keep the sidewalks clear for our mailman and passersby and of the wet messy boots on my kitchen floor and my dogs' wet fur and paws. I do have some very fond memories as a young girl enjoying the winter. In my purple wall-papered bedroom, with white furniture and purple shag carpeting, I had a clock radio on my nightstand by my pillow. These were the two ways I would find out whether school was cancelled or not: 1. My Uncle Mike Capitano worked as a supervisor for 35 years for the Pennsylvania Department of Transportation. He knew everything there was to know about the weather predictions and road conditions. I would call him and ask his opinion about the roads being clear enough for school tomorrow, as if it was going to be his decision to cancel school at Wyoming Area School District! But I was ten years old and he was, in my eyes, the expert. 2. My clock radio was set to WARM 590 (an AM station) for the announcements for school cancellations and delays. Not that there were many cancellations when I was in school, but when there was...woohoo! Then I would quietly peek my head into my parents' bedroom and tell my mom that I didn't have school that day. And back into bed I'd crawl. Eventually I'd wake up, a little later than the usual 6:00 am, and after dressing, making my bed, and having breakfast with Mom and Dad before he left for work, my snow day would begin. When I was very young, it was all about playing in the snow with my friends on my street. We built snowmen, had snowball fights, attempted to build igloos, and ate lunch. As I got older, my chore was to shovel and clean off the car and I did this without hesitation. I even shoveled the sidewalks of the neighbors to the left and right of us. But, when that was done, I was off to meet my girlfriends. We didn't care how cold it was; we wore our boots, stocking hats, mittens and ski jackets (not one of us skied, but it's what they called the water repellant, insulated jackets). I had an icy powder blue one with a white and gray fox fur trimmed hood. My parents gave it to me for my birthday one year. I loved that coat; it was a White Stag. We thought we were the cat's meow, as Carmelita would say, cheeks a rosy red and toes numb, but we didn't care. It was a day off from school and we were going to take advantage of every minute.

Today at work, my coworkers and I were talking about the snow, and a few of them were putting on their boots before we left. We all carry our boots in a plastic grocery bag. My thoughts wandered back to the days in elementary school when my mom, with all her goodness, bought me what she called a "shoe bag." It was a red faux leather case with a hard plastic handle, and it was big enough to carry my shoes in. It looked like a mini suitcase. Her logic was for me to wear my snow boots to walk to school and change into my school shoes. We had coat rooms in those days so it was easy to store my case and my boots. She told me it wouldn't be good to keep my boots on all day because my feet would be sweaty and I would get athlete's foot. I didn't even know what that was, but God forbid I should get it! So I carried my shoe case to school every day that it snowed, and I swear I was the only one who did that. Bless her heart, always thinking about what was best for me. I told this story today at work, and guess what...not one person knew about the shoe case. Well, wasn't I special?

❦ ❦ ❦

Last Sunday, I was off from work and decided to make a pot of homemade spaghetti sauce. I tried a shortcut a few times and bought jarred sauce and doctored it up myself, but honestly, it just wasn't the same. So I returned to my old way of making sauce like my mom. I bought five large cans of crushed tomatoes and a large bouquet of fresh basilico -- that's what gives it so much flavor. I don't use tomato sauce or paste; I like my sauce to be light rather than thick like gravy. I added some browned ground beef to make a meat sauce and I must say, it was delicious. A nice bowl of penne with homemade meat sauce, sprinkled with (well, more like a light coating of) pecorino romano grated cheese, and chicken cutlets make for a delicious traditional Italian Sunday dinner. As I made my sauce, I reminisced about how when I was a young girl, my mom and my grandmother Nellie canned fresh tomatoes. My dad always had a garden with a lot of tomato plants, not enough to can, but just enough for salads and marinara sauce for dinner. Dad was close friends with one of the owners of a family-run grocery chain, and he'd order a few bushels of tomatoes for my mom. I even remember going to a farm to pick the tomatoes a few times. The big canning ordeal would take place in our basement. We had two large stationary sinks to boil the jars in, a stove, and a large table to work on. The cellar door leading to the outside was left open for air to come in. I can just remember walking down the alley behind our York Avenue house, cutting through our neighbor's yard leading into our backyard, and all I could smell was tomatoes being cooked with a basil and garlic aroma! It was a big project for these two ladies. I can't even remember how many jars of sauce they'd can, but they lined a few shelves on our basement wall. There were enough jars for months, almost until the next summer. My Aunt Mary Lou and my mom would also make bread-and-butter pickles, small cucumbers sliced very, very thin, jarred in a brine and used on sandwiches. I can't imagine doing all this work today; I should have paid better attention and perhaps I could've learned. But I do know how to make my mom's sauce; we enjoy it and it brings back wonderful memories of her.

"Do as I say, not as I do." How often have we heard that saying from our parents or the older generation? My son is learning to drive. Only five more hours of practice, and he'll be ready to take the drivers' exam for his license. When he is with me, he does all the driving, and I kind of like being chauffeured. I talk a lot to him while he drives, teaching him the way of the road, I guess. I give him helpful hints on what to expect on our familiar roads and foresight on how to be a defensive driver. I have to say he is doing a really good job with it all. One thing I remember my mom and dad warning me was to never ever ever pick up a hitchhiker and to never take a ride from a stranger. Last week driving down Wyoming Avenue to school in the morning, there was a young man probably in his twenties thumbing for a ride in broad daylight on a busy road. It occurred to me that I had never mentioned to Philip about not picking up hitchhikers. I said to him, "And another thing, never pull over to pick up a hitchhiker." He looked at me, and I said, "Do you know what I mean when I call someone a hitchhiker?" Of course he did, but really I wasn't sure if he had. I guess I felt that way because he was never behind the wheel until recently and, just like he never paid attention to road signs and names of streets before (this is the kid that told me not to worry about him going to the Bloomsburg Fair because they were going to take route 17 when he really meant route 11), I figured he didn't take note of strangers trying to hitch a ride. This reminded me of a story of an incident that happened when I was about ten or eleven years old. It was Thanksgiving and we got a very unexpected heavy snowfall in West Pittston. The roads were nearly impassable. My parents and I had plans to have dinner at my grandma and grandpa Maira's house in Pittston. They lived on the top of East Oak Street in Pittston and the hill to get to their house was very steep. In fact, most of the streets in Pittston are hills which makes things difficult with snow. We were going to get there no matter what, and if we couldn't drive there, the next best thing to do was to walk. Any other time of the year, this would have been a very nice walk; I've walked from town to town hundreds of times even as an adult with my German Shepherds, but it was cold and I worried about my parents walking all this way. Mom packed up big grocery bags with the food that she was bringing to my grandparents, a bag for each of us, and we started out on our Thanksgiving journey. We walked from York Avenue to Susquehanna Avenue and then across the Water Street Bridge that crosses over the mighty Susquehanna River into Pittston, my parents' hometown. We were halfway across the bridge when a car passed us by at a little faster speed than my dad would have liked and splashed us with wet snow. Not to disappoint us with his stern personality, he yelled to the young man driving the car, "Hey slow down!" He also made a motion with his free hand to slow down. The car pulled over right on the bridge; he was the only car on the bridge at that time. I thought to myself, *oh God, here we go, this punk is going to get out and there's going to be a fight with my dad, and honestly I doubt my dad would even know how to throw a punch.* Instead the young man's girlfriend was in the passenger's side, and she rolled her window down and the man leaned over and asked us if we needed a ride over the bridge. My father, who always warned me about getting into a stranger's car, said yes, and all three of us, bags of food included, squished ourselves in the back seat of this young dude's car. Oh my God! Was my father nuts? This kid was so kind; he actually drove over side streets in order to get us to grandma's house. My dad handed him a few bucks, we thanked him, and that was it. In retrospect, I think the guy had thought my father was hitchhiking, the way he motioned with his hand. There you go, the old saying, "Do as I say not as I do," has its own meaning for me.

I've never been a fan of change, unless of course, it was change brought about by me. Change, as in cutting my hair, painting a room in my house a different color, or buying a new comforter for my bed. In general, I believe that if it isn't broken it doesn't need fixing. However, my life over the last eleven years has been nothing but change. Beginning in October of 2008 until July of 2011, my family lost a whole generation, the anchors of this family. My Uncle Mike Capitano passed away in October 2008, my Aunt Rose Maira in November 2008, my Uncle Tom (Skippy) Murtha in December of 2008, my dad in July of 2009, my mom eighteen months later in January of 2011, and her twin sister, five months later, my Aunt Leona Capitano in July of 2011. Gone, just like that. Some deaths were expected, while others were not. It left a void in all of our lives, and suddenly, we became the next generation to keep our family together. This is not a simple task. Some of my cousins, like me, have lost both parents, while a few of my cousins still have both or one of their parents with them. I often hear and I do witness families where a phone call is satisfying between a child and a parent but the actual spending of time is rare. I do not understand this concept; it is very foreign to me. I can't tell you how many times and how much I wish I could pick up that phone (yes I still have a house phone) to call my parents or get in my car and pick up Carmelita. I wish for those days more often than you think. We mourn because we lost those we loved, those that influenced our lives, and those that gave so much for us. We adapt to the change, but it is never easy. I've faced the changes in my life with plenty of tears, frustration, and anxiety. However, there will always be change, and we will always be forced to adapt. Things happen whether we want them to or not. My divorce after twenty-seven years of marriage was a huge change for me. I survived and I can talk about it now, but it's still not easy to totally accept, because it's not the way I had planned my life. But there have been many constants in my life that helped me cope and get through rough times: My family, my two aunts and all my cousins with their unwavering support and love were key to my survival. My devout and loyal circle of friends, old and new, without whom I don't know where I'd be today.

The one constant in my life that I really never bothered to think about was my profession. I am a Medical Technologist and I have been since 1988. Working in a laboratory has been my livelihood for all those years. Times are changing. Healthcare is changing, and in my opinion, not for the better. It seems to be all about the money, and patient care and standards are lowered, and hardworking health care professionals are not appreciated by these huge conglomerates. Their main concern is to constantly expand their market share and beef-up the competition between themselves. They buy up real estate and are always under construction. You'd think this would be wonderful for our economy wouldn't you? More buildings, more jobs, more employment opportunities. That's not always the case. In order to keep doing this, they need more money. Medicare is lowering their reimbursement funds every year, and outside contracted independent laboratories that hospitals send specialized testing to raise their fees. Where do they get the funds to keep doing this? Here's the answer: They begin a round of layoffs. Not layoffs for management, or vice presidents or presidents or directors. It affects the workers that actually do the work behind the scenes, the dedicated and hardworking individuals that make them look so good in the public eye. I suppose this is the business aspect of it, but for the average person like myself, it makes absolutely no sense, and they do not care. It's been explained to us that layoffs are to eliminate duplicity within the system and centralize certain functions within one facility to improve patient care. That may be good when the distance between facilities is nominal, but this is not the case. And what looks good on paper may not be good in reality. The centralized facility is two hours away from our entity. Within the next few weeks, my coworkers and I will find out our fate. It is extremely unsettling to have perfect strangers, a very powerful machine, making a decision about your career and how you earn a living while you have no control over their decision. I've been stressing about this, losing many nights sleep over it, and have a feeling of helplessness. But I realize that it's going to happen no matter how much angst it is bringing to me. I have been through many changes in my adult life, and this will be another hurdle to overcome. Whether I lose my job or not, it will be a sad day for all of us. Perhaps this is a way for me to expand my horizons and learn a new task. I have been enjoying writing this memoir, I just need to dedicate more time to it and try my best to publish. Maybe I'll have a future in writing. Those chosen individuals whom I've let read what I've written so far are impressed that I'm capable of writing and have had great enthusiasm for me to continue and see it through to the end. I have also become comfortable with public speaking, something that used to make me want to almost throw up when I was in school and had to read a report or a speech in front of my class. You know those speeches that you had to do…a demonstrative speech, an informative speech, a persuasive speech, etc. I hated it, but it was usually a required class. I also had written and oral communication classes while at the University of Scranton, also recommended classes. It wasn't until adulthood, when I was a lector at Church every Sunday for eleven o'clock mass for at least ten years, that I slowly overcame my fear of reading in front of a crowd. I did eulogies for a few family members, including my dad's, and I wrote my mom's eulogy but I couldn't read it; I asked my friend Father Paul to read it for me. I always say, if you can perform a eulogy, you can speak in front of a crowd at any time. So, perhaps if I lose my job after sixteen years at this facility, and thirty-one years in this profession, and I sure hope I don't, I think I may pursue a career as a motivational speaker; perhaps after I publish this book. If I talk to people about loss, change, family and communication, and I can help them to overcome hurdles when all seems to be crumbling in their world, it would make me happy.

My son is in his junior year of high school and the time is upon us to discuss colleges. He attends a college preparatory school that is doing an excellent job gearing him up for the years to come. He is blessed with a brain that allows him to excel in his studies, and I thank God every day for that. He thinks he knows what he'd like to pursue but is not one hundred percent positive. These are the words of encouragement I have tried to enlighten him with: Whatever profession you choose, you've got to love what you do so that you'll love getting up in the morning and love going to work; if not, it's not for you. That's not to say that you might love what you do for a time and then grow beyond that position. That's normal and means perhaps it's time for a change. And it's never too late to change your career path. Making a ton of money isn't everything in life. I reflect on the saying that money doesn't buy happiness; I'd want him to make the kind of money that means he doesn't lose sleep at night worrying about finances. I'd want him to be financially secure and be able to comfortably support himself and then a family -- and travel. I want him to travel and to see different places and experience other cultures. Traveling enriches one's life and I want to instill that in him. I have done my fair share of traveling and I hope to do a lot more before I die. I will try my best to continue to travel with Philip until the day comes that he no longer wants to travel with his Mom. I believe one of the biggest stresses we have these days is money and not ever having enough. I work every day I possibly could and yet the stress is there. I'm thankful for my blessings, and I realize that life is not easy for anyone. Each and every one of us has their own version of stress and hardship. As parents, we only want what's best for our children and we want them to have the best and perhaps have a life that's a tad easier than ours. This is my greatest hope for my son, my pride and joy.

❦ ❦ ❦

Sometimes I think a little too much about certain things. Sometimes I even let things upset me when it's really not worth being upset about. But I think that's human nature. Some people have the gift (and I truly believe it's a gift) to allow things to roll off their shoulders and keep plugging along with life. I often ponder about the roles of women and men in this world and how they can be so different. Women are emotional and men are cerebral. This is probably true for, oh I don't know, maybe eighty-five percent of the population. Women are the multi-taskers and men handle the task at hand. Neither is good or bad or one better than the other, just my observation and my experience. There are also specific expectations when it comes to the two sexes. Women, from the beginning of time through to the 1960s, were all about the home and the family. We still are at the present time but we've had to take on so, so much more besides the home and the family. I think as females, we were often seen as the weaker of the two sexes, and now we have no choice but to put on that brave face and be strong. In adversity, disappointment, sadness, change, and loss, I've had to reinvent myself to be a strong person. I work diligently to maintain my independence and my confidence level. It's not always easy and it's not always enough, but it's very important for me to do so. Maybe that's hard to comprehend, but if you know me, you understand why. I still believe in being a good person, a respectful person, a genuine person. I still practice being kind to others and being a support to my friends and family, because gosh knows they have all done the same for me. But is it okay for a strong person to feel defeated at times and feel like we are struggling to survive and get to the surface of the ocean wave so we can inhale and take in a deep breath? I'd like to think it is. It certainly doesn't mean I am weak again; it just shows that even the strongest people can have a bad day. Crying helps. It is not silly nor is it weak. It is a release for me and I prefer to be all alone when I do cry. Crying is a release of toxins...a cleansing of sorts. Cry, feel sad for a while, and then try to move on. I was never one to hide my emotions. Again, not good or bad, just saying how I am. I've been told I wear my heart on my sleeve and you can tell what's going on in my mind just by my eyes and my facial expressions. Yes, that's who I am. I think that makes me real. I have polished my personality so that I can speak my mind, express my opinion, and do what's best for me. Every woman has their unique way of taking care of themselves. Some go for spa days; some have a girl's weekend; others hire a cleaning person to tidy their houses. This is what I like to do for myself, sometimes nothing at all. I enjoy the quiet and peacefulness of my little house (except when my German Shepherd is barking at the postman), I enjoy a super hot bath with a glass of wine in my hand, or if the timing is right, a beach vacation. But on a daily basis, my "me time" is solitude. Being alone is nothing new to me; I'm an only child, and that's just the norm for me. It's rare with schedules to keep and responsibilities to tend to, but it's much needed and cherished. We need to take care of ourselves. We need to decompress and learn to settle down every once in a while. I'm getting older, and I can't keep going around in circles like a car doing laps at the Daytona 500. We need to realize that not everything has to be perfect and not everything must be done all in one day. The world will not end if I don't vacuum the house for two days (the dog hair will always be there, on the third day). It's okay to be five minutes late when I'm rushing from work in Scranton to Kingston for my son's swim meet. It's okay if my Visa bill goes out two weeks late; the CEO of Visa is not coming to the Oregon Heights section of Pittston looking for Tina Louise. And it's perfectly alright to order a pizza one or even two nights a week when there's no time feasible to prepare a home cooked meal. All these things used to be the old me and it was slowly killing me. I didn't know it though, I just thought this is life, and I needed to be the best I could be at EVERYTHING. I've learned and I've changed. I need to take care of ME.

❧ ❧ ❧

Many years ago, I heard someone had said of me, "She's living in a bubble." I believe I took offense to that remark at the time, but as time goes by perhaps I was. I had a certain way of conducting myself in private and in public, I never really expressed myself to too many people, and I guess I thought that my life was what it was. I can compare myself to a robot, repeating the same motions over and over and over. I looked at individuals and situations one way and only that one way. I accepted behavior and actions to be just what they were...actions.

Of course I always knew right from wrong, and respect was ingrained in me from my parents. Skip ahead many many years, and I've stepped out of that bubble and suddenly light has been shed on the way I perceive my surroundings. I can understand people and their behaviors so much more clearly now. I can see through people and the persona they portray for the public, leading a lonely and unfulfilled life. They surround themselves with similarly false characters in order to feel important. It's like I used to see life through those proverbial rose-colored glasses and now that I've changed my prescription everything is so much clearer now. I have come to understand body language and postures. They are so telling in all situations. I have become extremely attuned to behavior, and sometimes it's not good for me; it disturbs me and sometimes makes me sick to my stomach. Close talkers, talkers that cannot keep eye contact, talkers that sweep their surroundings with their eyes as if what you are saying is less important than who or what is in the room, talkers that feel the need to touch others while conversing, all telling of their personality and their insecurities. I have the gift of intuition, and at times it is so heightened that I can read an individual within the first few minutes of observing their moves or listening to what they're saying. I am right every time. What is even more unsettling is knowing that there was probably a time in my life that I was in that bubble with people of this nature. I may or may not have realized it then because it was my life and it was my norm, but now I feel uncomfortable just observing and experiencing this even for a very short time, minutes even. I just want to shout out and say "Wake up! Be real, get a handle on what you're pretending to be, and stop the falseness, you look like a fool." Wouldn't that be a relief to be able to actually say that to people? Unfortunately, someone is likely to take offense to that, which in itself says it all. To the same effect, these same people would have no problem telling you if that's how they perceived you. Expressing how you feel about a person, looking from the outside, telling them how they are being perceived, is a fragile task. So we don't do it, even if it's someone we know well. We hope for their sake they will see it in themselves, but most likely this will never happen. Since I've been on my own the past five years, I have learned a lot of new things. I have learned that people don't change. I have learned that most individuals want to be a big fish in a small sea. I've learned that people want to be known, seen, and feel important. I've learned that sincerity and being genuine are rare traits, although I do have people (as few as they are) that are both of these things in my life and I'm very grateful for that. My small circle of friends and my family fit this bill. John, the man in my life currently, also fits this bill. I think most of the people out there in this great big world need a reality check in their lives. I think those same people need therapy, too. It's funny how when life throws you a curveball, you must learn, you must grieve, you must accept as best you as possibly can, and you must change your way of looking at things, individuals and surroundings. This is me, this is how my life has been the last ten years, and I can only assume it will continue to be this way till I no longer breathe air. Other people's issues and the way they conduct themselves in public or wish to live their false lives are not my problem and the sooner I work on that concept, the healthier I will be.

❦ ❦ ❦

It's prom time here, and my son went with his girlfriend of four months. He looked so handsome and grown up in the new black suit I bought for him in November. And she looked so pretty, too. They are in eleventh grade. He went to his first semi in ninth grade but didn't have the greatest time. He was still awkward with the dancing aspect of it and the socializing part too. Last year semi was the same weekend as Districts for swimming so he did not go to that dance. This year he went. He had a great time! The dance was from 6:00 pm to 11:00 pm. They said there were no plans made for afterwards, and quite frankly I was thrilled with that. Then the text came at 11:05 pm. How opposed would I be if they, along with a few other friends, went for a "snack" at a chain restaurant that serves breakfast 24 hours. A snack? They just had a big dinner and dessert bar, but ok I get it. I said ok but please don't be very late. I tried my best to fall asleep, because I had work on Sunday and had to be up by 5:00 am. But, who was I kidding, I couldn't sleep. I looked at my clock at ten to one. Here was my dilemma: do I text him and ask where he was and how much longer he was going to be, or do I wait it out and let go of my apron strings a bit? Good thing I waited, because at exactly 1:00 am, her car pulled up in front of my house and he was home. Thank God! We only spoke briefly because it was late, and I told him we could talk all about it tomorrow when I got home from work and off to bed I went for four hours of sleep.

Thinking back on my high school days, and the days of proms and formals, I fondly remember this particular story I'd like to share with you. I was a sophomore, and a junior asked me to the junior prom. He was a tall, thin, blonde-haired, green-eyed young man who was on the track team. He was very soft-spoken and I believe a nice guy. I went home and asked my parents if I could go, and my dad did not answer. In fact, he didn't give me his answer until two weeks before the actual date of the prom. I remember telling Mom that the deadline for him to buy the tickets was up and I needed an answer. He said yes with this stipulation --

I was to come home immediately afterwards, at midnight. No galavanting around, no house parties or at that time, kids used to rent a motel room for the night and fill the bathtubs with ice and beer! There would be none of that nonsense with Sam Maira. He came to pick me up. He walked up onto my front porch and I was just coming down the stairs as he attempted to open the screen door; it was jammed. Yep, it was stuck. It took at least five minutes for Mom to get it opened. It was probably a sign that Dad was hoping I didn't go. But, after the traditional picture-taking, off we went. My best girlfriend at the time had a boyfriend (to whom she is still married today) who was also a junior so that's who we would be sitting with when we arrived at the prom. The evening went well; he was a quiet kid and so was I, believe it or not. I hadn't known him that well; we had a chemistry class together and that was the extent of it. But it was fine. Here's how the evening ended. My mother, because she was an angel sent from God, invited my friend and her boyfriend back to our house. She had prepared a banquet for us -- homemade pizza, all kinds of cheeses and pepperoni and crackers, dessert and coffee. She knew in her heart that Dad was strict, and she wanted to make me happy by entertaining my friends to let us not feel like we were missing out on a good party. Of course, she and the chief sat at the dining room table with the four of us and engaged in our conversations. And then it was done and over, my first prom with an older guy. I thought about this time in my life as I asked Philip about parties afterwards and he told me, "No mom, there are no plans." I understand plans come up especially when you're in a group, and going to Denny's for pancakes and bacon is perfectly acceptable. I know for sure that's where they went, because in the morning, I saw that he had emptied his pockets on the kitchen table, and his money and the receipt from the "snack" from Denny's was there. He is a good kid. He is kind, and he is genuine. I love him so very much. My how times have changed.

❦ ❦ ❦

Many people have been asking me about this memoir. The most asked question is where in my life am I. I say that it's not meant to give a year by year explanation of my life, but I incorporate events of my life along with inspiration, encouragement, and life lessons. I have lived fifty-five years to date, and I have thousands of stories to tell as would anyone else my age, but I felt the time was right for me to write it all down as a form of therapy for myself, and to enlighten my family and friends as to what I have lived through and dealt with up to the present day. I also hope my son will appreciate this autobiography so that someday he will see the person I am, other than just his mother. This writing thing is something all new to me. I never thought I'd be able to express myself so freely as I have. I'm even surprised at myself to tell you the truth. I had often laid awake at night, unable to sleep, with thoughts of just about everything going through my brain, when it occurred to me that maybe all these ideas would suit me better if I wrote it in a book-like format. I'm happy I decided to do just that. When I'm alone and my house is quiet, this has become my favorite thing to do. I'm not positive how I will finish or how much more I'll write, or how on earth one goes about getting a book published, but I know for certain that this has been a wonderful new hobby for me and I will try my best to see it through to the end.

I consider myself to be blessed in many ways. Fifty-five years ago I was blessed to have been placed in a family that loved me and gave me a wonderful life. I am blessed to be surrounded with a compassionate and giving extended family. I am blessed to be healthy, happy for the most part, and blessed to have the gifts of common sense and intuition. I am supremely blessed to have a son that makes me proud every time I look at him. And I am extremely blessed to have a group of friends in my life that I have come to depend on, admire, and love. The older I get, the more I realize that friends are such a vital part of our lives and bring such enrichment to our existence. My circle of friends are caring and giving individuals who have stood by me when I thought my life was not repairable. When I thought I wasn't going to be able to pick up the pieces after losing my parents and my marriage, Frank and Kathy, who have been in my life for oh so many years, really were my pillars. They were there to listen, to give sound advice, and to make sure I didn't spend too many evenings or weekends alone. They looked after me and included me in everything, as family members would have done. Frank and Kathy gave me strength and confidence to go on living. They made me realize that I have wings to fly. My friend Susan, who has certainly endured heartache in the last few years, more than anyone should have to face, has remained a constant in my life since 1984. She never faltered in her friendship with me and I know that I can rely on her for anything. She and her husband Mike, the best man in our wedding, never picked sides. She was mature enough to know that what I needed through the divorce was a confidante and true friend to talk to, and she was it. Frank and Kathy and Susan play a special role in my life, and I thank them with all my heart. Along the way, Sally, who was once just an acquaintance, also became a very dear friend. Sally, having gone through a divorce many years ago, could relate to all the emotions I was dealing with. I look at her and I admire her strength and tenacity. She is a successful businesswoman, and I believe she is genuine and is the real deal.

As time passed, I reunited with an elementary school friend, Donna. She convinced me to attend meetings with our classmates (class of 1981 from Wyoming Area), and it's been five years now and it's been the best thing I ever could've agreed to do. We have a steady group of a dozen or so class friends, and we spend so much time together that those from the other classes think we are crazy. However, we genuinely enjoy each other's company. There's no fakeness, we are honest and down to earth, we are so past all that high school drama of trying to impress, and we are who we are. Honestly, although I knew these people in school, I really did not "know" them. We were a large class, 318 or so, which made it difficult to be friends with everyone. But these past five years have been so comforting for me. We get together once a week and have gone on some pretty fun adventures. I was once a young girl who thought I only needed one best friend; now I'm a mature woman who realizes that I can have more than just one or more than three best girlfriends. All my girlfriends are best women. I don't know what I'd do without them.

Having male friends is just as important, but certainly on a different level. Each one is in a different circle, but each one is a part of my happiness. These friends, male and female alike, have been by my side through all the changes that I have faced. Changes that include happy times, sadness, disappointment, joy, and even crazy times. I know I can count on my friends to be a shoulder to cry on, and believe me I've done plenty of that and I'm probably not done! They are there to give advice and sometimes even tough love. They have shown me that life goes on even after grief. They have shown me that laughter, fun, adventure and hope are vital to us living a full life.

I have listened and learned from all of my close friends. I admire them all and have so much respect for each of them. These individuals have never left my side and some new friends (or shall I say old friends that I had lost touch with for many many years) have proven their allegiance to me and I will always be thankful for them.

❦ ❦ ❦

Camping. I can't say I've done much camping, nor is it my favorite thing to do; I prefer a week at the beach instead, but I have camped a few times in my younger days. Twice I camped with the Girl Scouts; one year we were in cabins and another year (the year of Hurricane Agnes in 1972), we were in tents. One particular camping weekend was spent in the Poconos. My Aunt Mary Lou and Uncle Jimmy had a camper kept at a campground called Indian Acres, not all that far from home but far enough that they felt they were getting out of Dodge for the weekend. One summer, they decided to take us kids to this campground for the weekend. My aunt and uncle and my mom and four kids; myself, cousins Jimmy, Tammy and Amy. It was fun because we were all together. We didn't care how we looked because no one knew us there and we were camping…camping is not a fashion show. We wore sweatshirts with mismatched pants, sneakers, and ponytails on our adventure. We couldn't just rough it though, so my mother brought a pot of sauce and meatballs; she was the best. What did we do without television or a phone? We had good old-fashioned fun. They had a community pool there, so of course that was a must. They had a gift shop a few miles down the road. I'll never forget its name, Blueberry Hill. It was full of country-like souvenirs, just what my aunt and mom liked. They ooed and awed and we were told to not touch anything! So typical. Back at the campsite later in the weekend, my cousin Jimmy and I had a friendly game of wiffle ball, with a bat that was the width of a two by four piece of wood called the Fungo Bat. My mom had brought it for us to give us something to do. So, we had Tammy (three years younger than me) and Amy (six years younger) in the "outfield," literally just a few feet from the camper; Jimmy was up to bat; and I was pitching. I was pitching because, afterall, I had a career in girls' softball in West Pittston for all of one season -- definitely not my cup of tea. Jimmy says to me, "Get ready T, this one is going to go far!" I took a step forward, wound up with the little white wiffle ball in hand, and went for the release, straight to him. However, the ball that was supposed to go far, also went straight, straight into my nose. That's right. Bang! Ouch! My eyes teared up, my nose throbbed, and blood dripped down my upper lip onto my chin. "Mom!!!" Good thing my aunt was a nurse -- ice to the rescue. I've mentioned that my mother was addicted to taking pictures and had a camera with her at all times; whether it was the old instamatic with the square bulb on top or when she moved up with the times and had a 35mm, she absolutely loved taking pictures. This weekend adventure was no exception, and she'd take pictures of anything, I mean anything. Believe it or not, Carmelita took a picture of MaryLou emptying the portable potty from the camper with Amy, all of about six years old, watching so intently. I'm not sure how she stood the smell! I came across these pictures not too long ago and I sent a snapshot of the picture from my phone to my three cousins, and we enjoyed teasing Amy about it. Laughter, fun, family and memories are what life is all about.

This past week, I attended a funeral mass for my great aunt Mary. She was the youngest of my grandmother Nellie's siblings. They were eight children with my grandmother being the eldest. Now that generation of Baiera's are all gone. I have wonderful memories of her and spent quality time with her when I was younger. At mass, the priest spoke about grief. He told us that grief is real. He told us to allow grief to happen naturally, let the tears flow and take as long as we need to accept loss. This is something that I can particularly relate to, and I have given this same advice to others that I knew were going through the grieving process. A time-frame cannot and should not ever be put on how long one should grieve. If it takes a long time, then so be it. Grief comes in all shapes and forms. It can be due to a death, a divorce, a lost friendship, loss of a job, or whatever causes your heart to break. No one has the right to tell someone to end their grieving period or just accept and move on. "We must allow ourselves to grieve," he said, and, "if we don't, it literally will make us sick." I agree. Speaking for myself, my most profound grief was from losing my parents, especially my best friend, my mom, and my divorce. A piece of my soul died with each of those things, and a part of my heart died, too. I'm not sure if I will ever be the same, but I am trying. I am definitely a different person in the way I look at the world, relationships, and life in general. My attitude has changed and my personality has matured. But even with those changes, I'm still not quite a whole person. There are days I feel empty inside. I feel a bit colder than I once was, and I ask myself if I will ever heal one hundred percent. I sure hope so, but it's taking a long time. I have no one in my life putting pressure on me and that's a great feeling. I am in control of my own emotions and if I'm still melancholy over losses, that's ok too. Recovering from grief is a long and sometimes lonely road to travel. It's an extremely difficult emotion to explain to a friend, especially if that person has not gone through what you've gone through. However, everyone has and everyone will at some point experience a broken heart. The time it takes for us to heal is crucial to our well-being. Some days I honestly feel like my heart is numb. This certainly does not mean I don't show affection or love for others close to me, because I am the opposite of that. I love to hug, kiss, and listen to others, and I show emotions of all kinds on a daily basis. My heart will never love anyone as much as I loved my mother; no one could ever take her place or give me the unconditional love that she gave me. I loved my family, the idea of marriage, my ex-husband, and growing old together while raising a child and then taking care of each other as we looked forward to making plans for retirement. Although I know no one can take Carmelita's place, I do know that love does happen again. There can be more than one love in a person's lifetime. There can be a new relationship with someone special. I have my doubts whether or not marriage is necessary to feel complete again, but that does not mean we miss out on the experience. My grieving has gotten better, and I laugh and I love again. I just need time for my soul and my heart to heal.

That morning, at mass, Father also talked about Aunt Mary having lived ninety-seven years and all the world events she lived through and experienced -- all the wars, the women's rights movement, and working outside the home. He also talked about how many stories she probably had to share with her children, grandchildren, and great-grandchildren. I understood his point, that telling stories of our lives is important and enriching. He encouraged her children to tell those stories to their own children and grandchildren. I sat there nodding my head in total agreement. This is why I decided to write down my stories and my beliefs, my words of encouragement and my experiences. I hope one day those who read this will understand.

I suppose if I am ever asked for advice, after a time of loss or grief, my words of wisdom would be to let yourself go through the grieving period, no matter how long it lasts. Allow yourself to cry and feel the emotions that come with a loss; whether it be a death, a divorce, loss of a long time friendship, a job, or whatever. Don't let yourself or anyone else convince you to move along quicker than you feel is necessary. It's a stage of life, and you are the only one in charge of your emotions. It's perfectly okay if no one understands but you. Secondly, I recommend reaching out to family and close friends. Don't be a hero and pretend you can do it all alone. I have found out, and thank goodness I did, that family and friends are vital. But, also, spend time alone. Don't alienate yourself from those that love you and want to support you, but it's not necessary to be doing something every minute of every day. Give yourself some alone time to gather your thoughts and emotions and get your life together. Allow yourself the solitary time you need to come up with a plan and prepare yourself for the journey that awaits you, no matter how different it will be compared to what you planned it would be. Alone time is pertinent. I do it once or twice a week; like tonight, I've been in my pajamas since 5:30, and I'm setting this time aside to write. Life is very busy, and we all need to make time to be alone, if that makes any sense. I take this time to think about my emotions and how I will face the next day.

Do not be afraid to ask for help. Do not be embarrassed to call a friend or cousin and have a good cry. Do not think that what you are going through isn't as terrible as what's going on in this crazy world today. If you are facing hard times, it's just as important. This does not make us weak. It shows we are strong enough to lean on a loved one when we need to. I have specific people in my life that I know I can lean on, and I thank God all the time for them. Find yourself those people, keep them close in your life and give yourself the space and time you need to heal.

❦ ❦ ❦

The other day I was reminiscing about my grandfather Louis B. Tuttilmond, or Papa Tutt all of us grandchildren called him. I know he came to America from Serradifalco, Sicily, as a young man and married my grandmother when she was just about sixteen years old. I can only remember him having a vending machine business, but I was told he worked for a company called Federal Yeast at one time. His famous words to my mom were, "Carmelita, I'll tell you what we're going to do today." In his later years, she was his driver, taking him to Dunmore, PA where he filled vending machines with products and emptied them of coins. This was a half hour trip on the highway in his light blue 1967 Plymouth, with push button gears on the dash, AM radio, and absolutely no power steering. This car was given to my mom after he passed away, and I'm ashamed to say this, but when she would pick me up occasionally from school, I'd tell her to park down the block. It was such an old car, I was embarrassed. The vehicle I currently drive has the same push button gears near the dash. The salesman tried to explain this concept to me and all I had to say to him was, "This is not new technology; my grandfather had this in his car fifty years ago." He told me another customer told him the same thing. The old saying that history repeats itself is true. I remember going with the two of them a few times, sitting in the back seat, no seat belt. I would stick my little hands in-between the back of the seat and the back cushion, because there were always coins in there that had fallen out of the drawstring bags after emptying the candy machines. I was lucky to find a few dimes and nickels. In my grandparents' cellar, Grandpa Tutt had a little office to the right of the cellar steps. It had a desk and some shelves with boxes of candy hidden behind a makeshift curtain my grandmother hung. On his desk was a big manual cash register that us grandkids just loved to play with after he had passed away. We played "office." His ledger and pencils were kept neatly in a drawer. He had recruited my second-cousin Lenny Coleman to help him count the coins and roll them in paper wrappers he got from the bank. Lenny also took him to his locations when Mom wasn't able to. Those candies are hard to find these days...Mary Janes; Chuckles, those soft jelly candies with sugar on top (they were in a long strip of five or six, all colors and flavors); Life Savers, in wintergreen and fruit flavors, but they were not called "Life Savers" -- the company name was Reed's; and the soft caramel candies with the white, almost marshmallow-like centers called Caramel Cremes.

Every once in a while he'd give me one. As kids we probably thought this was our own personal candy store and we had just hit the jackpot. That old cash register and those shelves stayed in that little house on West Oak Street in Pittston until my grandmother's passing when the house was sold. I'm not even sure what happened to the register, but it brought us a lot of fun when we were young.

❦ ❦ ❦

A few weekends ago, I spent my Saturday and Sunday painting. I love to paint. Dad loved to paint, and he showed me how at a young age. Our home on York Avenue West Pittston was built in 1925 and was a wood-sided house with shaker shingles at the top. Dad probably painted that house three times until he was unable to do it alone and had to hire a painting service. I have a picture in my baby photo album of Dad high up on a ladder with a paint can hanging from a rung on the ladder and a paintbrush in his hand, smiling for Mom and her camera. He gave me the chance to learn by painting the concrete blocks that were the foundation around the perimeter of the home. I guess he figured I couldn't screw that up, and no one would see it even if I did. With a brush and a can of Benjamin Moore, the rest is history. "Always buy Benjamin Moore, Tina Louise; it's the best." And I do. I've painted so many times I've lost count; I find it relaxing and a sense of accomplishment when my project is done. Some people think I'm crazy, but we're all a little crazy.

❦ ❦ ❦

It's 2019 and the other day while I was driving down Main Street in Pittston, my mind began to wander as I observed our little town and all the new changes that have taken place over the last twenty years or so. I still remember the "old days" in Pittston City, and it was pretty nice then, too. We had plenty of shops on both sides of the street and I probably shopped in every one with my mom. There was The Kiddie Shop, Starks, The ABC Shop, Nathan's, Waldman's, The Boston Shoe Store (I remember my mom buying me a pair of saddle shoes when I was in sixth grade in that store; it was on the corner of Main Street and William Street), Elaine's (what a beautiful store that was; the owners were very close friends of my parents and they had "high class" clothes in there;

later on, as a teenager, I would babysit their grandchildren). Leed's also had beautiful clothing for women and was owned and operated by a woman and her son; this man Charles ordered my wedding gown for me from New York. I bought my first denim jacket in Cohen Brothers; it was a boys' jacket, or as my mom would refer to it, "an Eisenhower jacket," but that's what we were wearing in those days. I think that term describes a waist-length jacket and probably has absolutely nothing to do with President Eisenhower! I remember strolling through Borr and Casey drugstore that sat on the left corner of Main Street and William Street, as you were coming down William Street; it had old-fashioned wooden floors that would squeak when you walked on them and really high ceilings with big old ceiling fans. Down the block from Borr and Casey's on the same side of Main Street was JCPenney's. Mom worked at JCPenney's in her younger days. She was the window trimmer and made all of the signage in the store for the sales. When I was a little girl, we would often go to JCPenney's and shop. The kids' department was way in the back of the store. A friend of hers still worked there, and every time we'd go in, this woman gave me a piece of gum. Her name was Marie, and she had black hair and was always behind the counter in the women's section. That structure eventually burned, like most of the old buildings on Main Street in the years to follow, and now a parking lot is there in its place. We also had F.W. Woolworth's and S.S. Kresge's on the same side, and the women working there were all dressed the same in a uniform. They wore an aqua collared dress with their name tag beneath the collar. My Dad worked with a gentleman named Scottie in a department store in Wilkes-Barre called Lazarus. Scottie's wife worked in Kresge's. Her name was Elsie, and she wore her hair in a high doo on top of her head. I would always see her there. On Saturdays, if I had slept over my great-aunt Grace Baiera's house the night before, she and I would walk downtown to Kresge's and she'd buy me a coloring book and crayons, my reward for helping her dust. Mom bought me my very first pair of 14K gold earrings when I was eight years old in a jewelry store in town called Wick's. Her cousin Leona Baiera (Mendelssohn) pierced our ears and we needed to buy "good earrings," so that's where we went to buy them. It was in that same jewelry store that Aunt Grace had bought me my first watch when she was my sponsor for confirmation in 1973. It was a SEIKO with a black strap, and she even had it engraved on the back with my initials in script: TLGM, Tina Louise Grace Maira. I still have it somewhere in my jewelry box. She loved me. There was an Italian deli called Mancia's, and in its place presently there is still a family-owned deli with Italian specialties. I remember going there with Dad to buy the "good pasta" -- that's what he'd call pasta made from semolina wheat, because the other brands were all "like cardboard." In the back of this deli by the meat counter were these big barrels filled with Italian olives. All kinds of olives floated in water with a big ladle so you could scoop some into a container. Quite frankly, they stunk. But the old Italians, Dad and my grandfather Joe included, loved them. The butcher in Mancia's would cut your meat as you ordered it.

We also had five movie theaters in town, but by the time I was old enough to go to the movies I only remember one, the American Theater. My cousin Jimmy and I would go see a movie there on a Saturday afternoon. There were restaurants, too. A few of them are still here today. As the years passed, many of these beautiful stores began to close their doors. They either went out of business for financial reasons, or they burned down. It seemed that a fire was nature's way (or perhaps, not nature's way) of closing a business on Main Street until the little town of Pittston City looked like a ghost town. Right around the mid to late 1970s through to the 1980s, a new concept emerged in the business world of merchandising -- the mall. The first mall I had ever gone to was The Viewmont Mall in Scranton. "All the way in Scranton." What a great idea; a bunch of stores all under one roof. But this was chain merchandising, and the family-owned shops in small towns like Pittston were about to become a memory. My dad had a men's clothing store at 16 South Main Street in Pittston, too, way before my time. He was in business for about thirteen years. The first establishment was on North Main Street, but he moved to South Main in 1948. When he closed his store, he went to work in the men's department at Lazarus's, a larger store in Wilkes-Barre. He was working at Lazarus's when they adopted me.

Many years later, Pittston is back. We have had a very ambitious mayor, Mike, along with a group of influential individuals who have had the vision for the past twenty-five years or so to bring Pittston back to its former glory, or maybe even better. Some of our neighborhoods still leave a lot to be desired, but our Main Street and our reputation emerged from oblivion. People from out of the area have great things to say about our town. We've got a beautiful streetscape with new street lamps framing our sidewalks (the same lamps I used as a persuasion to convince my cousin Amy to move back home from California), underground wires, new sidewalks with stamped concrete crosswalks, and trees lining the Main Street and Kennedy Boulevard. There are a few new restaurants and shops, and housing in historical buildings are in the making. Yes, Pittston, the Tomato Capital, is looking good.

It's been a few weeks since I've sat at my computer to continue my saga. I'm not sure why I haven't written but perhaps I've just been too busy with work and getting my house and outside ready for the summer. Summer is here. It's mid June, but you wouldn't know it. We've had copious amounts of rain since April and the warmer sunny days have been few. It's raining right now, so I'm taking advantage of this time to put my thoughts down on paper. So, I've been trying to record some of the more vivid events of my life and talk about my family and friends, my losses and disappointments and my joyful moments, as well. This is not an easy task. I can't make this memoir a thousand pages long; that

would be grueling, although I probably have enough material to do so.
This idea started out as a compilation of my younger years and my
experiences, so that I could leave something for my son to have and to
understand who his mom is and what she stood for, but it's become so
much more than that. I've incorporated past and present events and
feelings and I hope someday he realizes that I am a good person with a
loving soul and a giving heart. I hope he knows how much I love him,
because he is my whole life and I would do anything for him. I have tried
my very best to be strong for him, especially after his Dad and I divorced.
Also, not so easy all of the time. He's seen me at my worst and my best,
and he's been a great support for me...we support each other. When I
began writing this, these were my intentions, to be a recollection of my
life and connect some life lessons to them. Now, I'm not so sure what
this will turn out to be. In some ways it can be a self-help book to support
others that have gone through similar life events, or it can remain as a
diary. Perhaps it can be both.

My cousins have been and always will be an integral part of my life. I'd like to tell you just a little bit about who they are.

My cousin Tommy (named after his dad, Thomas Murtha, aka Uncle Skippy) is the oldest of my cousins. A man whom, even in my childhood years, I looked up to and admired. He was a great athlete and played football for Pittston Area, number 34. Tommy lived with my grandmother Nellie for the last two or three years of his high school years because his parents had moved to Mountaintop, PA. Living with grandma enabled him to continue playing football and to graduate from Pittston Area with his friends. As a young girl, I spent a lot of time at my grandmother's house, and going there at that time was a new experience. There was a lot happening there, with his high school friends always stopping over. My grandmother loved to feed them and now there was a stereo with rock and roll music playing! Never a dull moment. Tommy is a very hard-working man. He has been in the supermarket business since his college days and has worked as a manager almost his entire career, working long hours and managing many employees. He is a kind, respectful, and honest man. A husband to Sheila for many, many years, a father to two beautiful daughters, Jennifer and Jessica, and now a grandfather of four. Tommy has a great sense of humor and when we would all get together, we'd look to him to do hysterical impressions of some of "Pittstons' finest." Our town has had its share of characters, and we crack up hearing his portrayal of them. Tommy is a family man and I admire him for that. We don't get a lot of time to spend together, but I know he's there and if I should ever have the need to call upon him, he'd oblige. I'm thankful to have him in my life.

My cousin MaryEllen, the next in line for my cousins, has been my idol all my life. As a little girl, I looked at her as someone to aspire to. She was a cheerleader, a member of Pomeroy's Teen Board, on Homecoming Court, and always always dressed fashionably. MaryEllen has certainly been in control of her own life, leaving Pittston in her early twenties to work in Chicago; then on Holland America Cruise Ships as a ships nurse; meeting her husband, a Dutch navigator on the cruise line; and living abroad for 33 years. She and Ernst have raised three handsome, respectful, intelligent, educated young men -- Ernst, Samuel and Thomas -- while moving every few years all over the world, it seems. I've talked about her in my previous pages as someone who has been there for me after my mom passed away and through my divorce. She has managed to be there for me while living in third world countries and only coming home twice a year.

My cousin Michael (named after his own dad, Michael Capitano) is the same age as MaryEllen. Michael attended Pittston Area schools as well, and then went to college for criminal justice. He has worked for Pennsylvania Power and Light for his entire working career. Michael married his high school girlfriend, but after a few short years, the marriage ended in divorce, a devastating time for him no doubt. However, in the next few years, he met and married the love of his life, Maureen. They have an unwavering marriage and a devoted relationship. She makes him happy and they have always had harmony. Michael is a traditional man, believing in family values, and the center of his attention is always Maureen and their beautiful daughter Maria. He always checks on me via text or phone call to make sure I'm okay. Thank you Michael. Michael, Maureen, and Maria reside in his parents' home, which they have managed to make their own and honor my aunt and uncle by keeping the home in their family.

My cousin Louis (Louie, I've always called him), named after our grandfather, lives next door to his brother, my cousin Michael. Louis is the most talented man I know. Even at a very young age, he was always building something, "bunks" mostly, but honestly, he knows so much about his craft that he could build a home from the foundation up. He has worked in the construction business his entire adult life, is a master at this profession, and has always had an impeccable work ethic. It started with a newspaper route when he was eleven years old, fibbing to the newspaper company about his age because he just wanted to earn money. Always the funny guy at our family gatherings, he makes us laugh until our stomachs hurt and we get tears in our eyes listening to stories of his childhood antics. I love him like a brother, always have, always will. He is married to his junior high school sweetheart Gloria, and together they have raised a beautiful red-headed, intelligent young woman named Kristen, my godchild through Confirmation. I could call him out of the blue and I know he is there for me no matter what the circumstances.

My cousin Jimmy (named after his dad and his grandfather James Fitzpatrick) and I are only three weeks apart in age...I'm older. As children, we spent much time together, it was always an adventure, whether we were making plans for a long walk down to the quarry by his house on Chapel Street in Pittston, or a picnic lunch in the woods, or playing with his matchbox cars in the dirt under the pine trees in his backyard. I did the boy things because I just loved being with him. His mom, my Aunt Mary Lou, has told me the story about when she was preparing a nursery before Jimmy was born; while she was showing my mom everything she had for the upcoming arrival, my mom broke down and cried. Her baby sister was expecting a baby and she was still not a mom. Jimmy was born on January 7, 1964, and little did these two beautiful women know that on March 26, 1964, the newest arrival...me...would be waiting at the Luzerne County Courthouse. Jimmy has been through some emotional times too, but he's so fortunate to have reconnected with a childhood friend and after all these years, has married her. Donna loved him since grade school and now they share a life together. Donna is a wonderful stepmom to two very impressive young adults, Jimmy and Kate. Since my divorce, Philip and I have been included in holiday dinners at Jimmy and Donna's, and I'm very thankful for that.

Tammy Ann, my redheaded, curly-haired, crystal blue-eyed sister from another mother; she is always a constant in my life. Tammy is that one person who will always have a smile on her face even if things might not be so sunny. She is a strong woman but not a hard woman. She is kind and giving and always lends a listening ear. I admire her tenacity to learn new things and to step out of her comfort zone every once in a while. She looks at new ventures with enthusiasm and in such a positive way. She is crafty and exhibits such patience with everything she does. We are only three years apart, yet I felt like a big sister to her, from sleepovers, teaching her to drive, helping with homework, school projects, and school shopping, to being pregnant with our sons at the same time. She was the maid of honor in my wedding. We tend to see things with the same perspective and if not, we appreciate each other's advice because it's given with love and understanding. Tammy is married to Andy and together they have raised a sweet, handsome, very athletically-inclined young man named Adam, who will also be graduating high school in May 2020.

The youngest of my cousins, and of the eight grandchildren of Nellie and Louis Tuttilmond, is Amy. Amy is another redhead, but with green eyes and a strong-willed disposition. She is the take-charge one and never afraid to step out of the box to take a chance. She is my baby cousin, one that I always felt I had to look after and take care of (don't know why I felt that way; she has wonderful parents, but it came naturally to me to want to take care of her). I have realized recently that she is a grown woman, and I have to step back. She has the personality that can handle any situation with a brave face and a strong resilience that is to be admired. I loved being surprised when I came home from school and she was at my house. It was the same routine every time: my mother made her go into the laundry room right off our kitchen and hide so she could come running out to surprise me. I'd walk into the kitchen and act surprised when she came popping out. "Surprise, TT!" She was probably three or four years old at the time. We are six years apart. Amy has had her unexpected changes and heartaches in her own life as well. She handles adversity differently than I do. She's very strong, but I think it's a survival thing. The last nine years, since her return to Pittston from California, she has proven to be an exemplary mother. She has been raising three wonderful, respectful and intelligent children by herself, while working tirelessly to provide Nicholas, Noah, and Bella with a stable and loving home. She has found love again, with Mike, her husband of one year and four months. I'm happy for her. I hope she knows just how much I love her. My Amy Fitz, she always will be.

On my father's side of my family, I have two first cousins, a son and a daughter from my Aunt Rosie and Uncle Joe.

My cousin Charles (Charlie) was a very active child, they have told me. He was born in Trenton, New Jersey and lived there throughout his formative years until moving here with Aunt Rosie, Uncle Joe, and his sister Tina Marie around 1973 or so. Chas was a catcher on the baseball team for Steinart High School in Hamilton, NJ, and after moving to Pittston, was a wrestler on Pittston Area's wrestling team. He was somewhat serious, so as Tina and I were growing up, he was the target of our abundance of teasing. He took it well, and often his comeback was to imitate Donald Duck; he does a great impression! Charlie is very intelligent and precise and puts his heart and soul into everything he does. I think I've read where this is a trait of being left-handed, which he is. He attended Boston Architectural College and is presently a very successful architect in his own firm having an office in Princeton, New Jersey and Manhattan. Charlie introduced me to such greats as Jim Croce, Cat Stevens, Blood Sweat and Tears, The Beatles, and The Grass Roots. This was the music blasting in the basement of their Highland Hills home as he worked so intently on his latest design project. While in school in Boston, he weathered through many blustering snow storms, the kind when everything shuts down -- schools, transportation and businesses. One such time, he took the time to write me a letter. When I opened up this odd shaped envelope, I realized that this was not an ordinary letter. He had written it on this thin sheet of paper that measured over four feet long! I kept that letter in my desk drawer for many many years; leave it to him to think of something so quirky. I have the utmost respect for my cousin Charlie. He too has had to weather many emotional storms -- not just the ones in Boston, and he has managed to maintain his dignity through it all. He loves me, and he worries about me these days. I love him in return.

Charlie has a sister, my cousin Tina Marie, named after our grandmother Tina Flores Maira (my dad's mom) like me. Tina Marie and I are about seventeen months apart in age. She has the curliest blonde hair, fair skin, and hazel green eyes. I was a very picky eater when I was little; my mother had to cut the crust off of my peanut butter and jelly sandwiches. My aunt Rosie would say to me, "Crusts will give you curly hair just like your cousin Tina." Maybe I didn't want curly hair! I was so stubborn. My parents and I made many trips to Trenton to visit my cousin Tina and Charlie. When I was old enough I stayed there for a week at a time in the summertime. Our days were filled with playing dolls, riding bikes, and making cookies in Tina's Easy Bake Oven. Aunt Rosie and I dropped Tina off for her flute lessons in the morning. Simple things made us happy and we had fun no matter what we did. Tina often tells me the story of when Aunt Rosie finally told her that I was adopted. She didn't believe it at first, and then her natural reaction was to simply cry. We have an extraordinary bond. She is the most generous, loving, and kindest woman I know, always giving so much of herself to everyone. I said it before and I'll say it again, Tina has a heart as big as Manhattan and it's made of pure gold. Tina and her husband Joe have raised three wonderful children, to whom they give their heart and soul to, Carly, Joseph and David. They are the very proud and loving grandparents to three adorable grandsons.

Although there is so much more that I can tell you about my first cousins, I wanted to paint a picture of how blessed I am to have these ten individuals in my life...my brothers and my sisters from other mothers and fathers. This is the simplest way for me to describe how I feel about my cousins. Each one is special, unique and has left a footprint on my life.

🐾 🐾 🐾

I lived with my parents for twenty-four years, from adoption to marriage. However, I lived with my ex-husband for twenty-five and we were separated for two years before the divorce was final, but we were working on trying to repair the marriage for those two years, so legally I consider myself to have been married for twenty-seven years. We dated for four years before getting married. All in all I was with him for thirty-one years. That's a long time. Even today, I look at couples I know that have been married for a much longer time, some even for forty or fifty years, and I wonder to myself, *how do they do it?* Sure they probably love each other and respect each other, but they must also really have to work at it because life is so full of challenges, some expected and others that are not. They are committed to their spouses and the marriage and their family. I admire them, but I'm not so naive to think they don't have issues. How a couple chooses to deal with their issues is unique to them. It's a possibility that they stay together because they simply don't have the energy to start over. Perhaps they sacrifice their happiness in order to keep their family together. I'm really not sure what the right thing to do is anymore. I used to think, when I'd hear someone complain about their relationship or marriage, *oh, just suck it up and deal with it, there are children involved and it's about them not you or your spouse.* I thought that unless there was some sort of abuse, you stick with it because you made a promise to your partner. Presently, we live in a world where the practice is to focus on doing what makes YOU happy. We hear that unless you do what's right and satisfying for you, you'll never be happy or be able to be strong for your family. I think maybe it's a little bit of both and there's a fine line between being a better person for your husband or wife or life partner and just being selfish and self-absorbed. And if you're not careful, it could be a disaster if done to either extreme. And for those who do not see gray in their life, only the extreme ends of the continuum being all white or all black, it is definitely a slippery slope. There must be a middle ground, the gray zone. Similar to dieting, everything should be in moderation. Too much of a good thing, too fast, can be fatal. And in contrast, too little or if lacking in certain aspects is lethal too. My Dad told me, "Even if you eat lobster every day, eventually you'll get sick of it." Moderation. We live in a world where we desire immediate gratification. I am guilty of this from time to time. When I start a home project, I can't just do a little bit here and there; I have the need to finish it, even if it means hours and hours at a time. In my younger days, if I wanted that dress, I got it. I didn't wait to save up the money, just used the good old American Express and bought it. I wasn't to the full extreme like some but I still have a little of that in my personality today. When I got married, I wanted it all to be perfect. I wanted to always feel loved and to give love. I wanted quality time, inspirational time, intimate time, and a closeness with my husband. I strived to make delicious meals and keep a spotless house. I wanted to be admired by my family, my in-laws, and my husband. I wanted to be the best mom a child could ask for. I suppose I wanted it all, and why shouldn't I have it, if it's in reason?

Some of how I live my life is just because of who I am, and the rest is how I was raised. I wasn't raised to be selfish or egotistical or disrespectful. But now I try to think of myself and what's best for me, without short-changing the important people in my life. It's not easy. It's a delicate balance that I struggle with every day. I now have a wall up for fear of being hurt again, and I'm afraid of giving too much of myself and losing myself again. I'm not sure if that will ever go away or if it's a bad thing. I gave so much of myself that somewhere along the line, I was living for others and not for myself. I didn't know the gray zone. The biggest hurt of my life thus far has taught me to care about what I want and what I need. What's hardest now is for those close to me to try and understand where I'm coming from.

I hesitated to write about the biggest part of my life, my marriage, because it is so full of memories and feelings that it will undoubtedly be the most difficult passage thus far. I can't write about everything we experienced together because I would be old and gray by the time I finished. Oh wait, I *am* old and I take care of my grays every five weeks. Thirty-one years with the same person leaves many many pivotal moments and unforgettable memories, too many to put down in writing.

We met in 1984 at the University of Scranton, I was in my junior year and he was a sophomore. I had known him to see him and knew his name but did not actually know him. Walking into a philosophy class that September of 1984, I sat in the middle of the rows because I was never one to be right up front and noticeable. He walked in and sat towards the front but clearly in my eyes' view. I said to myself, "Well there's one person I kind of know from Pittston." I took notice of his gorgeous sweater and the perfectly fitting jeans he had on. His smile was wide, and his teeth were perfect and white. On the third or fourth day of this class, our professor suggested we pick our permanent seat so that he'd be able to match a name with our face. This was my opportunity. I saw where he was sitting and I moved up closer, close enough that we could have a conversation in the days to come. He smelled so good, he wore Paul Sebastian, a cologne that could only be bought at a higher end men's store at our mall, The New Leaf. I started off by introducing myself and told him I recognized him from the shoe store where he worked and as a lector at my grandmother's church, St. Rocco's on Oak Street in Pittston. Every class we exchanged pleasantries and eventually found out that we knew a lot of the same people; our towns were small and everyone knew everyone.

I'm not sure how long it was before we would meet at the Student Center on campus to exchange notes for class and study for exams, but that's how it started. In the months to follow, I knew I had to make a decision, and eventually I ended my four-year relationship. The next four years we were a couple. We did everything together. We had friends that we spent a lot of time with, we were both very comfortable with each other's family, and we had the same interests and likes and dislikes. We were good together. He picked me up on a Friday night, walking up my front sidewalk on York Avenue with fresh flowers wrapped in a wet paper towel and aluminum foil. My in-laws had a tenant, Elda, at the time who loved to garden, and she had beautiful flowers growing in the backyard. He used to pick some and bring them to me. I loved that. Some days during the week we had the same break between classes. His Mom would make us chicken salad sandwiches, and we'd eat in the parking lot behind the student center. I wonder if he even remembers these things now. After we were dating a few months, I made a mistake that I lived to hear about for the next twenty-five years. A young man in my chemistry lecture class asked me to go to the movies one night. I accepted. I don't even remember the logic behind my thinking, but I was young and stupid. I was nineteen or twenty at the time, dating my boyfriend for a few months, and yet I lied to him and went out with the other young man. What was I trying to prove? What was I thinking? I have no answers, except that I made a mistake, and I was never forgiven for it. We fought about it and broke up for a week or two. Obviously we got back together, but it remained a sore subject in all the years to come. I regret what I did. The next four years we matured, finished our higher education, graduated from The University of Scranton, and began working. In 1987, we got engaged at twenty-three years old. As I think about it now, I don't even know how we decided to get engaged. Some of my friends were already planning weddings, and we attended a few. I used to wonder when it would be my turn, and hoped I wouldn't be the one that was engaged for years before finally getting married. Sometimes I think it could have been me who put the pressure on, and maybe he wasn't ready. I can't be positive. It wasn't a surprise engagement, nothing romantic. I picked out the diamond from a friend who had a jewelry store in New Jersey and we had the setting made to fit the stone, and the wedding band too. It was beautiful. I don't even remember the month we got engaged -- I think it was June -- but the wedding was just about a year away, September 17 of 1988. My parents had a small gathering of my aunts, uncles, and grandmother, and his parents and sister Lisa at our house to celebrate. Our families sort of knew each other before we even met because, again, we live in small towns.

I was marrying the man I loved. The man I wanted to live the rest of my life with and have a family with. We planned the wedding for months. It was going to be perfect, and except for the rain that day, it was. It was at a beautiful venue, and all two hundred and forty-eight of our family and close friends were there to help us celebrate. We went to Maui for ten days for our honeymoon, our first trip alone together. There were one or two opportunities to go to the beach together when we were dating and even when we were engaged, but my father would not allow it. We spent the two months prior to the wedding painting and sprucing up the half of a double block home we were going to be renting in West Pittston. We lived there for five years. We were big shots, two young kids in a gorgeous three-bedroom home. I was very comfortable there, and very happy. We both worked full-time Monday through Friday. We spent quality time with our best friends, Mike and Susan, and life was good. It was an adjustment to go from living with our parents until the day we got married and suddenly being on our own; we were adults now. But that was life, and how we grow. We depended on each other, we supported each other, and we learned from each other. We were in charge of our own finances and learned very quickly that money is made and money is spent, and the vicious cycle continues. I used to say that those first five years were the happiest years of my marriage, until of course the day our son was born, almost fourteen years after we got married. That undoubtedly was the happiest day of our lives. Up until that point, our life was all about us. We did what we wanted, we went where we wanted, and we had no curfew. For me, it was a huge deal; I had a curfew living at home with my parents.

We moved into our forever house in 1993. This house was built by my husband's grandfather and grandmother, and his uncle had remained here until he retired and moved to North Carolina. The house was offered to us, and we bought it. We worked hard that summer to make it our own. We painted, installed new carpeting, tore out the existing kitchen, and updated it with everything new. I planted flowers everywhere I could find space, and we made good use out of the front and back porches. In November of 1996, we bought our first dog, a gorgeous German Shepherd, Sascha. Sascha gave us eight adorable puppies when she was three and a half years old, and we kept one female, Malca. They were our children. We had already been trying to conceive but with some heartaches. We had yet to be successful.

It was a good life; I cannot say otherwise. My ex-husband is very successful at his job, and other offices in Philadelphia and Washington have a high regard for his knowledge and his work ethic. He is a g[r]

, for us

person. And I was happy and content at my job. We had a lot

e friends.

-- young, successful, healthy, great families, and wonde[r]

ying our

We were happy in our little house on Elizabeth St[...] on a Saturday

needs as we saw fit, living for ourselves, fre[e]

and drive to Philly for the day, go to the beach in the summer, drive to

Clearwater in the winter to see my mom and dad, and spoil ourselves

with the best of everything. I loved our life. I loved being his wife. I only

wished he knew how much I loved that. I hope someday as we grow old,

apart, he can reach into his heart and realize my love for him was real and

genuine; I don't think he ever did, and that is a real shame. Perhaps if he

did back then, we wouldn't have divorced. I firmly believe that. Then in

2002 when Philip was born, well, he made our lives complete. Al is a

wonderful dad to our son. I know he loves Philip beyond belief and

makes him a priority. Never, did I think that my life would be turned

upside down. It's been five years now that I've been living alone, except

for the days and nights my son is with me. A lot has changed. There are

many times I feel anxious about my future and how I will face it as I

grow older. I have no answers yet, but I must remain strong and believe

v ability to live my life. I have made mistakes and I am far from

per. ut more importantly, I have learned from my mistakes. Granting

forgive a humbling act. I would like to be forgiven for mistakes I

have mad n trying to forgive those who have hurt me over the years. I am sure as the years roll by, I will make more mistakes and not so smart decisions, but I am trying really hard to live a good life.

❦ ❦ ❦

My cousins are always telling me that they can't believe how much I can remember of our lives, and friends have told me I am a great storyteller. I don't know why I can remember so much, or perhaps it just seems like a lot when I just remember the tip of the iceberg. I think it's because I genuinely have so many fond memories that I reflect on my life with a sense of happiness and love and closeness to those in my life. I had lunch last week with one of my dearest girlfriends Susan. We reminisced about how our lives used to be. We asked each other, why did our lives have to change? Susan's twin sister Carole passed away just a few years ago. We talked about our times together, the three couples, and how little did we know that Carole would leave us so young, and I would be divorced, and our intimate circle would be forever changed. We had tears in our eyes remembering happier times. Life sometimes can be cruel. Life can be challenging. Life changes lives, if that makes any sense. We learn to adjust, we accept, and we continue on this journey. But, never do we forget what we had.

Last month, I went on a bus trip with John to Little Italy, in New York. It was the Feast of San Gennaro. This is a week-long celebration held on several blocks of Little Italy. All the restaurants and bakeries have stands out on the streets, and tents are arranged with tables and chairs for dining. It is crowded with so many people, so many Italians! It was a beautiful day, warm but overcast, and thank goodness because with the crowd and the warmth, if it had been sunny, it would have been uncomfortable. We arrived there around one o'clock in the afternoon and the bus left Manhattan at ten o'clock that night. I looked around and memories flooded my brain, memories of the many trips Dad and I made to New York, always making our way to Mulberry Street for dinner, and the times we stopped in at his favorite delicatessen and bought sopressata and salami and a loaf (or two) of fresh Italian bread to take back to Pittston with us. Nothing there has changed. The restaurant we always ate dinner at on Mulberry Street was still there, and packed with people inside and outside under the tents. John and I tried to get in for dinner, but the wait was an hour. We went down the corner to another place, and it was delicious. Before leaving, I stopped at a vendor who had Italian cookies -- fig cookies, biscotti, anise cookies, etc. I bought an assortment to take home. Just standing in line looking at all those delicious cookies, while the salesperson weighed cookies on a scale for the customers before me, reminded me of my dad's love for fig cookies, his "cuccidati." My mother made them for him a couple of times a year; it was a special treat. He bought a few packages of figs which she ground up in my grandmother Tina's old metal grinder. She'd make the cookie dough from scratch, again, a recipe from Grandma Tina. They were a lot of work, but it made him so happy. He gave Mom suggestions though, "Use half the amount of sugar, Carm. They don't have to be so sweet. And don't use cinnamon; I'm allergic to cinnamon."

The cinnamon thing is another story… He told everyone he was allergic to cinnamon. I even sat as he told an anesthesiologist who asked before surgery, "What meds are you taking, Mr. Maira, and do you have any allergies?" He replied, "Yes, I'm allergic to cinnamon." I looked at the doctor; he looked at me. "Dad, you are not allergic to cinnamon."

"Yes, I am." "Dad, have you ever gone into anaphylactic shock by eating cinnamon?" "No, but when I eat it, it gives me agita." Indigestion is not the same as an allergy. He used the cinnamon allergy as an excuse forever; my mother couldn't put it in her apple pies or her cookies. Sam was Sam.

As a kid growing up, I never liked the fig cookies. My mother's Toll House cookies were my favorite. I think Dad was glad to have his cuccidati all to himself. Mom would store the fig cookies in Charles Chip cans, layering each with a sheet of wax paper in between to keep them fresh. After dinner every night, they'd have a cup of coffee. My mother always had cookies made. Her motto was that you always had to have something to go with the coffee, so she baked almost every day. As soon as dinner was done, dishes cleaned up, and the coffee pot on. Sam meandered over to the cellar door and down a few steps to the landing where she kept the Charles Chip can, and you could hear the can opening. And he'd come back with three little fig cookies in his hand, enough for only him. We'd laugh, because he'd say to me, "I feel really bad that you don't like these fig cookies." "Yeah, I know Dad." Enjoy your "cuccidati," Dad.

I am slowly realizing that life is a continuous cycle of change. I know I've talked about change already, mostly when it dealt with my life and the changes I've faced, but also generally speaking. Presently our world is experiencing climate change, political change, and economic change. People feel the need to express themselves with such force, oftentimes an angry force. Who are we all mad at? When did we become such an angry society? Anger brings such anxiety and ill feelings towards one another. Then, when we're all "angered-up," we look for solutions. We become the "all about me" crowd. This mindset in and of itself is unhealthy. Frankly, it's not all about us, individually. I still feel anger within myself due to my vision of how my life was supposed to be and how it has actually turned out. Yes, live your life. But do so without alienating family and friends.

We have become such a busy society that finding time to spend with the ones that you love becomes a luxury. My time is limited. I work a lot of different hours at my job and the schedule I keep is hard even for myself to keep track of. It seems nowadays, I have less time for my friends and I miss them a lot. I work this schedule out of necessity. I'd much rather have a normal 9 to 5 occupation, but at fifty-five years old, I'm too old to start over at a new career. If I could just win that damn lottery that I play every week, all my problems would be solved. I am fortunate that my close circle of friends are always there for me; most understand the reason for my work habits, while others have told me I'm not living in the moment because I'm too worried about my future. Someone has to worry about my future; it may as well be me. Nevertheless, I value the people in my life. They may not all understand or agree with how I'm living, and that's ok. I can only do what I think is right for me and my life in the years to come. I know we can't always plan the future, but I cannot sit by idly and not prepare.

I am a dog lover. I had a small black terrier mix when I lived at home with my parents; her name was Pepper. My friend's dog had a litter of puppies, and my mom fell in love with one of them. Dad was not so much a dog lover. He was going to Italy for two weeks, and that was when my mom decided to pick up the puppy and bring her home. My father was gone an hour, and she and I were already in the car to go get Pepper. We brought her home and attempted to house train her in the two weeks he was gone, as we knew we had better do that quickly before Sam Maira came home. We put her in our laundry room by the kitchen with a window screen up to block the doorway. We knew absolutely nothing about raising a dog. When Dad returned two weeks later, he walked into the kitchen and heard the puppy whimpering. He looked at me, then at Mom. "What the hell do I hear?" My mother said, "Well, Sam, we got a dog." I thought he was going to blow a gasket. He asked what her name was; we told him "Midnight" because she was all black. He said, "That's a dumb name, how about Pepper? That's black." And so it was, Pepper was a part of our family.

When she was house trained, she chose to sleep with me every night, either on my bed or on my bean bag chair. Yes, I had a big, lime green bean bag chair. It looked so nice in my lavender bedroom. Pepper was the boss, as small as she was. She only weighed about eighteen pounds. She never ate dog food; my mother gave her leftovers every night. She was a companion to me, but she only liked us. She was not a lovable dog; I don't believe terriers are lovable. She had a nasty streak, and we unfortunately had a few incidents when she snapped at a few people, which ultimately was her demise after eleven years. I never thought I would even have a dog, because my mom had bad allergies; we always thought she'd have a difficult time with dog hair. She did not. And she loved that damn dog. She was the one home all day with her and gave her a lot of attention. Pepper was often the subject of teasing. My cousins liked to tease her, until one time she bit Louie's big toe and tore a hole in his sock. We laugh about it now, but I don't think we laughed then. She was nasty, and she wasn't the prettiest looking dog, but she was my pet, my only pet other than a ten gallon fish tank that I had when I was in elementary school. I was in college when we had to put her down, and I never got another dog until after I was married.

In 1996, our trainer at the gym convinced us to buy a German Shepherd. A big dog? I knew nothing about this breed nor did I know how to handle a large dog. We bought her anyway. A gorgeous female, whose parents were from Germany, she was born here in Dallas. We named her Sascha, after her great-grandmother. She was powerful. Large for a female, and very dominant. The first year she gave me a hard time, challenging me. I took her to obedience classes, and she soon realized I was her friend, and then she became our protector. She had a job and she did it. She was traditional in color, red and black. The red was a dark amber color on her ears, head, and neck. The rest of her was jet black with some beige on her hips.

She was almost four years old when we bred her to a magnificent male named Flash, owned by Diane, a woman who quickly became like family. She imported Flash from Germany, and he had a wonderful disposition. Together, these wonderful dogs gave us eight beautiful puppies in June of 2000. We were well-prepared, read books, and watched VHS tapes on how to deliver the babies and what to do afterwards. Between 10:30 am to 11:00 pm, eight puppies were born right in my TV room. Sascha had six females and two males. It was a wonderful summer. They were a pleasure to watch grow and develop their own personalities. It was a ton of hard work, I'm not going to lie, but well worth it. I kept one female; we named her Malca, a Hebrew name that means "Queen." She was the one that always wanted to be by me, the first one to stand up in the whelping pool when I walked into the room, and she loved to cuddle on the couch at night with me. Never did I think we'd have two big hounds in our little house. After eight weeks, every time an owner came to pick up their puppy, I would cry. I had four puppies left after thirteen weeks, so I thought I had better pick one before they were spoken for, and Malca was the one. Sascha was a great mother, always caring for her babies, and never neglected them.

We spent the entire summer having our family and friends over to play with the puppies. I wanted them to be handled by adults and children to prepare them for their new homes. And when our guests left, Sascha went to each one and licked the tops of their heads. I'm not sure if she was counting them all to make sure they were all there, or washing them from everyone holding them. I have this entire experience on film. Not that long ago, I connected my old VCR to my television, and John and I watched the film. It was so refreshing to see those beautiful little puppies moving about and whimpering, learning to stand up and eventually play and interact with their littermates and with us, and with the plethora of family and friends that spent sunny summer weekends here at my house and in my yard playing with them. What an absolutely wonderful experience it was. I thought perhaps I would do it again one day, but now is not the time. The many fond memories, both in my head, and in photos and on video, will have to suffice.

I am experiencing some level of anxiety and or depression presently. I have come so far handling all the changes, but every once in a while, reality rears its evil head. Memories from the recent past invade my brain like a virus. Such a thing is happening right now. All it takes is a spark to ignite the fire within my brain, and such a spark brings back all the anger and sadness and disappointment I've had to deal with. This spark was ignited this past weekend, and now I'm left to deal with my issues again. The flame that burned my house to the ground is still smoldering; she's still clouding the streets of my town; she still has control over my emotions because I see her as "danger." This flame has no idea the damage and scars she has created. Hopefully, no one else, married couples or otherwise will ever endure the danger she presented to my life and my family. They say Karma always comes around, so I can only hope that karma will douse the flame that destroyed my house. The time has come to face that flame.

My divorce was a trauma. This came about after a time of several deaths in my family, including my parents within eighteen months of each other and my second mom, my mother's twin Aunt Leona, only five months after my mom. Two years later, the death of my marriage. I hadn't the time to grieve from one death to the next. But something goes off inside of me when the reality of my divorce is brought to the forefront, and I'm down for the count for a few days. I've stepped on one or two people's toes this week by getting feelings off my chest, and I've more than likely made hard feelings. Hopefully this time will pass and I can continue to heal. It's taking a long time, years, and I am intelligent enough to realize that. Time shouldn't be my major concern here. Recovery in my situation has nothing to do with being book smart; it's matters of the heart I am dealing with. I've been told I am angry. Some people have told this to me in not such a loving way and others did it out of their concern. Yes, I'm angry. I'm very angry. Divorce bred anger in me. I was not an angry child. I was brought up in a very loving home. I was not an angry teenager. I was not an angry young adult, adult, wife or mother. I am, however, an angry divorcee.

Want to know what else divorce does? It teaches you to mistrust. I was always a trusting person. Maybe I didn't trust strangers on the street, but once you entered my life, I trusted you. Now I hardly trust anyone. There are maybe four or five individuals that I trust one hundred percent; others are on a sliding scale of percentages. I find myself leery of men, generally speaking. I'm aware there still are good men out there with a true heart who are willing to commit. I believe John is one of those men. However, I still sense that a lot of men are untrustworthy. This, I've observed and learned. When word of my separation was made public, my phone was bombarded with texts and messages from men curious about me, perhaps a bit too curious for their own good.

Divorce teaches you to build a wall of safety around yourself, for fear of getting hurt again, before the first wounds are even healed. This wall prevents me from giving all that I used to give or am capable of giving for fear of losing myself to others and having the wind knocked out of me when I least expect it. It's a survival tactic. I am incapable of giving myself to others in ways they expect. I can't do it and I won't do it. I will lose myself if I do, and that's not healthy. Unfortunately, those that still love me will not understand this change unless they too have gone through the same hurt. Divorce brings insecurity and fear of the unknown every single day. It brings fear of the future. I can admit I'm scared, although I have no idea how to remedy it. I rely on my therapist.

The only good thing about divorce is that it has improved my eyesight to see the true character within people. Some say this is being judgmental; I say it's being safe. I'm seeking genuine people to share my life with, but in this small town that I reside in, genuine people are a rare breed. It's mostly about being seen and being in the right crowd. I am so over this mentality, or maybe I'm just in a bad mood. I don't need to be told to "let it go"or that I need to move on, or I'm so strong or that this will kill me. I've been told by my therapist that the scars I bear will always be within me, and what I should try to do is to learn to live with them and try to move past them. I must accept these scars because they will forever be a part of me. My brain knows this is true. My heart is not communicating with my brain at this time. I know they tell me this out of love and concern, however what I really need is "your feelings are valid," " I will try my best to understand where you're coming from," "you can count on me," and "I'm always here for you to vent." This is what I really need. This is what's valuable to me. I don't need advice from untrained individuals; I will get the advice and tools I need to move past this from a licensed therapist. What I need from family and friends is love and support, expressed with kindness. This is what has become of me post-divorce. This is certainly not the way I was raised, but it's the way I'm raising myself.

❦ ❦ ❦

In April of 2009, we made the heartbreaking decision to put to rest our German Shepherd Malca, the pup of Sascha's that we kept for ourselves. She was suffering from the same disorder as her mom, Degenerative Myelopathy. It's a neurological disease common in large breed dogs, where the myelin sheaths coating their nerves start to disintegrate. Sascha was eleven years old when we lost her to this debilitating disease, and Malca was two months shy of her tenth birthday. It's genetic, passed on from one of the parents to the puppies. Genetically speaking, it is almost identical to MS in humans. Sascha and Malca were paralyzed from the hips down, scooching along, dragging the whole lower half of their bodies. We carried them everywhere with a padded sling with handles, out to the yard, onto the couch, up two flights of stairs to bed at night and down the stairs in the morning. We lifted them up into the back of our vehicles for vet appointments and used the sling to carry them inside. With Sascha, I sought out a veterinarian who practiced holistic medicine and took her for acupuncture every Wednesday, hoping to give her some relief. They told me she was not feeling much pain, because she was numb. Maybe I was looking to make myself feel better knowing I was doing everything in my power to make her feel better.

One March day, I carried Sascha out to the yard. It had snowed and was cold. When I tried to slip the sling under her back legs to carry her back into the house, she curled her lips back and showed me all her teeth, something she had never done to me before. I knew she was done. After a struggle she moved a little on her own, using the strength of her upper body, and we slowly walked back in the house. With tears in my eyes and a heavy heart, I made the call to Dr. Edwards. The next morning, Al and I took her in and let her go in peace, a horrible day. I had Malca for two more years before I noticed the signs of DM with her.

When she stood up from a down position, her two back legs were entangled and it was a struggle for her to separate them. My heart broke. With Malca, I did more reading about DM and decided I would follow a natural diet I read about. I stopped commercial dog food. I cooked large batches of food that lasted for about 3-4 days at a time and gave her ten different supplements and vitamins from the General Nutrition Center. It gave us another year with her.

Linda, a coworker of mine, had a German Shepherd that would be delivering puppies in May of 2010. I knew I would eventually get another dog, but after losing Malca, I thought I would give myself a break from being a canine mom. One day I made plans to take Philip to see Linda's puppies when they were around five weeks old. My son, who was eight years old at the time, walked up to the puppies, picked one up and said, "Ok, this is the girl for me." I didn't go there to get a dog. Linda had discussed with me a few times that she wanted me to have one of her pups. She knew how I had loved my dogs, and that she would have a loving home here. I left there with no commitment. I arrived home and an hour later, I called Linda and said, "Ok, we will take her." Best decision ever. Elsa will be ten years old on May 26, 2020. She is healthy and still jumps on my bed and fetches a ball like she's two years old, and I thank God I still have her. She is all black, with dark tan legs and black toes, so different from Sascha and Malca. She is my companion and offers unconditional love every day. She is my protector. I'm never fearful of being in my home alone. She's my baby. I will be lost without her someday, but for now, she sleeps side-by-side with me, on the couch and on my bed, happy when her back is against my back -- all eighty-four pounds of her. Thank you Linda and your family for giving her to us.

❧ ❧ ❧

We will make a million promises in our lifetime. As children, we promise to behave in church or at a restaurant. As students, we promise to do our homework in a timely fashion. As young adults, we promise to appreciate and respect our parents and our family, and to be responsible. As adults, we promise to do everything...to be on time, to make your favorite chocolate chip cookies, to be there for our friends and family, to get home from work early to watch our son's baseball game, to be honest with one another, etc. When we get married, the vows we exchange on that altar are promises. We promise to love one another, in sickness and in health; we promise to be true to one another; we promise to be there for one another in good times and in bad times. Then why is it that fifty percent of the human population breaks these promises? There's an old saying, "Promises are meant to be broken." I never understood this. If you can't follow through with the promise, simply don't make it. They were not meant to be broken. When promises are broken, intentionally, it brings hurt, sadness, disappointment and resentment. Understandably, things happen that cannot be avoided, like having to cancel dinner plans or a trip, promising your child a certain video game but finding out you didn't preorder it and now it's sold out, things like this. Some promises should never be broken. Life is hard enough. We face challenges on a daily basis and make vital decisions all the time; some will change the chartered course of our life. Work together as a team. Communicate. Trust one another. Grow together as partners. Keep the promise you make, as long as it is a healthy one.

The other day I was thinking about the winters that I would visit Mom and Dad in Clearwater, Florida. I spent two weeks with them getting away from our cold, harsh winters in Pittston. Two weeks on a beautiful beach or poolside was always just what the doctor ordered. They rented the same condo in a gated community in Largo, just fifteen minutes from Clearwater Beach. Sunshine and the beach was Dad's version of heaven. I laughed to myself because when I go to the beach, I intend to spend the entire day there. And mostly that's what I did, except on occasion Sam and Carmelita had their own ideas about what encompassed a day at the beach. Mom and I often went ourselves, just us girls, for some private quality time. Dad had many Pittston friends who had moved to Florida post-retirement so he usually met "the guys" for breakfast or lunch, and that was just fine with us. We set up our lounge chairs and covered them with a beach towel, lathered up our skin with sun lotion, and we were good! One time while she and I were relaxing, she turned to me and said, "See that beach hut over there? They have the best hotdogs. Let's go get one and let's have a Coors Light." Huh? So that's exactly what we did. We ate our hotdogs and drank our ice cold Coors Light on a picnic table under the hut for fear of the seagulls swooping down and stealing our dogs. On a different trip, Mom, Dad, my ex-husband, and I were all at the beach together. We rented a cabana so we'd have a break from the sun if need be. Around 4:30, Dad said, "Ok, let's pack it up. The Adams Mark Hotel has a happy hour at 4:30 and the beers are half price." I was beginning to think that my parents were all about partying while in Florida. There was a calypso band playing at the same hotel on their outside deck. Where there was music and libations, who were we to say no? When it came to going out to dinner, there seemed to be an urgency to get there by five o'clock. I soon realized the "early bird special" was a big thing for retirees in Florida. We had to stop what we were doing and get home to shower and dress, so we could make it to Leverock's, a restaurant right over the bridge from Largo to Clearwater Beach. This was the routine, a few dollars saved from the hours of five o'clock to six thirty was what their world was all about; I couldn't argue with that.

❦ ❦ ❦

Kind. Kindness. Kindly. We use these forms of the word kind in all different scenarios, and they could mean different things. Generally speaking, I think it has the same inherent meaning. It is usually the opposite of mean, it could express a gentleness, or sometimes it is used in place of the word "please," as in, "Kindly hold the door open for me." It's a gentler way to express ourselves. I like to use it in place of the word "nice," because it has a different tone to it. For example, "She is so nice." I prefer to say, "She is so kind." It has warmth to it. I think what our world needs today is a lot more kindness. I don't look fondly at people who feel they can say whatever they want, just allowing the words to roll off their tongues without thinking first, and then using the shield, "This is who I am; I say it like it is." I believe this attitude comes either from a person's hardships in life and the obstacles they have faced and survived or the fact that maybe our world is changing and this is now the norm. That just by saying this gives them absolution and a "pass," that it's okay and acceptable to say whatever they want. I don't think it is.

Just when I think I've experienced it all, just when I believe I can handle just about anything, just when I have the confidence to stand up for myself, the game changes. No one wants to hear constructive criticism. Even if it could help with the way they deal with others, or maybe be a gateway for me to understand why the atmosphere has changed so drastically. I never claimed to know everything, but with age and life, I have gained knowledge and wisdom. It may have taken a whole lot of heartache, sadness, and disappointment, but this has made me open my eyes to see life more clearly. I'm intelligent and I speak from my heart. It's the only way I know.

❦ ❦ ❦

In my therapy session today, my counselor and I discussed relationships. We talked about the fact that our parents never gave us a lesson on relationships. This could mean friendships, intimate relationships, work relationships, etc. No one told us what to expect or what we should be willing to give and get in return. She told me she's been married thirty-seven years and back when she married, no one was giving her advice. I told her I was in the same boat. As a young woman, I believed that if we loved each other, that's all we needed. Love is not the only thing we need for a successful marriage or relationship; in fact after the initial thrill and infatuation of it all, marriage becomes so much more. I think love is what gets you together, but from there it requires trust, respect, communication, understanding, empathy, and so on. She gave me an assignment: if she gave me $250,000 to build myself a new home, I certainly wouldn't just hand over the money to a contractor and say, "Call me when it's done." I would sit down with drawings and blueprints; I would decide how many bedrooms and bathrooms, design my kitchen, family room and porches, and then I'd decide what goes into each of those rooms.

I should treat my life like a blueprint for my next house. I decide what goes in those rooms...independence, financial stability, occupation, family time, friendships, romantic relationships, intimacy, fun, travel. I am in charge of building my own home. I don't have to ask anyone for help or permission -- been there, done that. I'm so glad she put this analogy in a way for me to think about and plan, because I have a fear from deep within that if I give in, I will lose my independent self. I can't let that happen. I've come too far. So there's an invisible shield that protects my body, mind, and my heart. I didn't intentionally put it there; it appeared on its own. The last five years, I've had to build my home from the ground up, take care of everything alone, and raise my son by co-parenting. This was a new world for me, a new home for me. Although challenges and anxiety can appear out of thin air, I'm comfortable in my life. I have to believe in myself and know that each day can be a new beginning. I often doubt my capacity to give my whole self to someone for fear of getting hurt, or to become dependent on someone. Maybe it's that, or maybe it's because I want to be in charge of building my new home. I will continue to be counseled, so that I can become an even better woman, an independent woman who will give of herself but not lose herself, a woman that can enjoy an intimate relationship without fear of a broken heart, and a secure woman who will accept the changes presented to me and learn to live with them.

❧ ❧ ❧

I grew up on a tree-lined street in West Pittston, York Avenue in a neighborhood of wide streets, sidewalks and old homes some over one hundred years old. The neighbors were friendly, and it was always considered to be a safe community. Children were free to ride their bicycles or walk to the little league field, the library, and the community pool. When families bought a home on this street and surrounding streets, they were usually there for life. I loved my home. I lived there until the day I got married. I was twenty-four years old. My Dad bought this house shortly after my adoption, and they moved in on Halloween night, 1964. I have nothing but fond and loving memories growing up in that home and in the small borough of West Pittston. I still have the deed and papers to that house. Dad had kept them all these years in the safe deposit box at The West Side Bank. After his death, I took them from there and I have kept them with all the papers that were in his possession. This all wood-sided home, with a large backyard and full size attic, was purchased for $13,000 with a $50 deposit! Despite a devastating flood in 1972, we were not leaving our family home.

When I was in fifth grade, we were burglarized. That evening I was with my mom at her sister Sara's house, where one of those home decor parties was taking place. Mom asked Dad to pick me up on the way home from work (he was working at Samter's in our mall) so that I could get to bed. It was a school night. He did. He and I walked into the house, and I went straight upstairs to my bedroom to get ready for bed. Dad went into the kitchen, and all I heard was a string of Italian curses. I

turned from the landing on the stairs and ran right down to the kitchen.

There he stood at the back door in the kitchen which led out to our lattice

back porch. It was a wooden door with nine square windows. The one

closest to the knob had been shattered and glass was on the floor.

Someone had broken into our home via the back door on the porch. He

looked at me with panic and shock in his eyes, and said, "Tina, we've

been robbed." I was really scared. He walked over to the kitchen phone to

call the police, but when he did, there was no dial tone -- these were still

the days of wall phones. Our phone was dead; the telephone lines on the

outside of our house had been severed. I suppose this was just in case we

had been home at the time of the break in, we would've been unable to

call for help. Hand and hand, we walked together upstairs to see what

damage had been done. My bedroom was untouched. We had a small

chest of drawers in the hallway, and the drawers were pulled open and

disheveled. My parents' bedroom door was shut, something they never

did. We walked inside the bedroom to find a mess. Dresser drawers and

highboy drawers were pulled out, and all my parents' personal

belongings were strewn all over the bedroom floor and bed. Dad knew enough not to touch anything, and we proceeded back down the steps, and then over to our neighbors', the Bullions. We called the police and they were quick to respond. There had been a few other robberies in West Pittston the past few weeks, but they had no luck finding the culprits. I was really frightened. Just the thought alone that strangers had been inside our home and rifled through our personal space and touched our belongings, and even stole some of our possessions, was very unsettling. Dad called Aunt Sara's house and told my mom to come home; my Uncle Skippy Murtha and my cousin Tommy came with Mom. Obviously we were all upset at what had happened. Mom walked me up the street to my best friend Maria's house where I would spend the night and go to school with her in the morning. The police were there going over everything, dusting for fingerprints and making out a report. Our things were never found and neither were the small-town thieves. For the next week or so, I was afraid to go upstairs to bed alone. I'd sleep on the couch downstairs until my parents were going upstairs too.

I suppose this event left an impression on my mind because I could picture it all happening in my mind's eye, like it happened last week. Safety is something we all need to feel. Living alone in my little house on Elizabeth Street, I often wonder what I would do if I heard someone trying to break in. I have had a German Shepherd in my home since 1996, and certainly that is a deterrent. When my ex-husband and I first separated, I worried that my son, who was only eleven at the time, might not feel safe without his dad being here. I tried the best I could to comfort him and assure him we were fine. If that meant sleeping in my bed for the first two weeks, then that's what we did. I assured him we had the very best personal protection dog there was and she would never let anyone come in to harm us. I was probably saying that to convince myself as well. We deserve safety in our workplace, safety in our churches and schools, safety in our relationships, and most importantly, safety in our own homes. There is so much violence in our country presently that the one place we need to feel secure is our home. Sometimes, that sense of safety is violated, just like it was that night on York Avenue, but we manage to become stronger and we soon realize that as long as we were not harmed, money and material things are replaceable. I am alive and well to retell these stories of my life, and for that I feel thankful.

❦ ❦ ❦

As an only child, I've grown accustomed to being alone and have become very adept at being comfortable with being alone. I feel an aura of peace when I'm alone and I'm never bored. I have a busy life, with my job and all the off-shift hours I work in conjunction with dayshift hours, trying to keep up with household chores, events with my son, and giving time to relationships. The time I may spend alone is necessary for me to regroup, rethink, and reevaluate my life. When else can I do this? At work, I must concentrate on what I'm doing for the health of the patients; at home with Philip I must be as present as I can be to be his mentor and support system and his role model; for my friends I must be just that, a friend; and for my intimate relationship, I must be a partner. This is certainly not a boring life and, perhaps two to three days (or nights) a week, I need to decompress. We all do, some more than others. I'm the "some more than others," though I can't say exactly why. Perhaps it's because I'm prone to be an overthinker. If I feel overwhelmed, I need alone time to have a good cry for myself. If I'm exhausted from talking all day at work, I need to come home and not talk. I think maybe a lot of women feel this way. We handle so much with work, family and our homes that we feel guilty for wanting to do absolutely nothing and just be anti-social for a few days. And this is absolutely ok. Taking care of ourselves is essential to our well-being. My advice to women and men, is to take time out to just be alone. Take advantage of me-time to clear your head of thoughts, sort through your emotions and breathe deeply to cleanse the stress and anxiety. We all need it, I know I do.

❦ ❦ ❦

As I embarked on this journey of writing stories of my life, my initial intent was to write a loose version of a family tree for my son, and to tell him stories of my childhood, my teenage years and my adult life. I wanted him to read about his Mom so he could see that I am more than just someone who cleans, cooks, and does his laundry. Somehow along the way, this book became so much more. It's a unique compilation of life stories with life lessons gently infused to paint a picture of my life. Not that I am anyone special -- I'm not a movie star; I'm not a political figure (God forbid); I haven't discovered anything scientifically important, but I'm a woman who's had to morph into a strong, independent, and outspoken individual in order to survive changes out of my control. I was raised in a very loving environment, a home that instilled respect, compassion, kindness and generosity. I had a very good life, and for the most part, I still do. My son Philip is my heart and soul. He amazes me every day. I have no doubt he will go on to be a successful adult and hopefully, he will practice the kind of life that his dad and I have instilled in him.

I had no idea where I would end up with this writing, but to me it's a healthy mixture of many things. It's my personal history, it's a diary, and it's therapy. I am not qualified to give professional advice; that's not my background, but neither is writing a book. However, my life challenges, experiences, losses, disappointments, joy, happiness, and thankfulness for what I have, have given me the wisdom to express this in words and share my life. Should this happen to help those who read it to overcome obstacles and maybe put a smile on their face or even a tear at the melancholy parts, then so be it. I began this adventure almost two years ago. I am now fifty-six years old, as of last month. I certainly have many more stories to tell and lessons to learn; perhaps that will segway into a second book. I might be writing it from Wesley Village Senior Living...

This I know for certain. I am healthy, happy, and appreciative to all those individuals in my life that have been there for me unconditionally and have not wavered in their support as I changed. I'm extremely thankful for Philip, for his love and his unique way of looking at situations, and his intelligent perspective that allows me to open my mind to seeing things in a different way, when I often felt I was losing my mind. Life is a challenge, but life is good. I'm able to get out of bed every day, and live my life as I see fit. I miss my mom and dad very much, and my heart aches wishing I could hug my mom one more time and hear her laugh, and ask my dad for advice and listen to him strumming on his Gibson, but I know they are with me and watching over me. They gave me a wonderful life, and now it's up to me to live the rest of my wonderful life.

If I had only a few words of advice to give to anyone who faced grief (which is any loss you experience, not just death, as we often associate it), it's that in the end, it will be okay...YOU will be OKAY. Respect your past. It will always be a great part of your life, but learn to put it in perspective; I'm still working on this part. Rebuild your "house," "decorate" it as you like, allow "visitors" that you choose inside, and don't worry too much about having all your plans in order. Change comes along at a time we least expect it.

Don't be ashamed or afraid to ask for professional help...there are a lot of people out there willing to give free advice about life and relationships but it's been my experience that they are not qualified to do so. Don't look to philosophers as your sole means to repair your issues. I studied philosophy at the University of Scranton; it was part of their liberal arts education as a Jesuit Institution -- I was "jesu-cated." In my metaphysics class, I studied Descartes, Aristotle, Plato, and Nietzsche. In real life, we cannot solely live our life based upon the writings and teachings of philosophers from hundreds of years ago, unless you are able to truly understand their teachings. We should follow our gut instincts and use common sense. The only exception I would make for this is Jesus' Ten Commandments; these are meant to teach us how to live and if we obeyed these commandments, the world would be an awesome place. They were not written to solve our emotional issues, but to help us respect each other.

Presently, it seems to be the fad to quote Buddha and believe we are living the life of kindness and understanding he wrote about. That's a wonderful gesture if we followed his ideas. Most of the time, this is not the way we are, and that's too bad, because the world would be a utopia if people were that genuine and kind. It's nice to read and have an instructor attempt to enlighten us and encourage us to be thinkers, but if we think these quotes and writings will heal our issues from within, we are mistaken. Perhaps these teachings along with professional therapy is the answer. Face your problems, knowing that people in your life are not the only ones responsible for your unhappiness. Stop trying to find fault with others in the present or from the past, blaming them for what is missing in your life, and desperately seeking fault with loved ones to excuse your actions. Own up to the real cause of your unhappiness. Look within yourself; most of the time, this is where the problem was born. Recognize the problem and then do yourself and your loved ones a favor and seek out real, qualified, educated help. You won't regret it. It is not a sign of weakness but strength.

I am not perfect. I have made mistakes, plenty of mistakes, and I have spoken out of turn, I'm sure. I should learn to let go of things that bother me and live for the day. I am stubborn in my own way; most of the time I think it's due to thinking my way is the better way or that I'm the only one that can do it right. I can't give up my way and go back to the way things used to be. It's probably a subliminal trait I've developed to maintain my strength and my independence. I am a work in progress. I figure I have about thirty more years to perfect myself, hopefully by that time, when I leave this planet Earth, someone will stand up at my funeral mass and say I was a genuine person. I'm trying my hardest to live a life that will bring me peace, love and happiness (and a little rock n roll, haha). It's not always easy and I know this because it was one of Mom's sayings, "It's not easy, you know." She was right. She did it all with a radiant smile. I can only aspire to be like her. I'm dedicating this book, in loving memory, to my parents, Sam and Carmelita, without them, I would not have these wonderful childhood stories to tell my son. I'm also

dedicating this book, in "living" memory, to Philip, my whole world.

Made in the USA
Middletown, DE
18 February 2022

61483071R00150